MIXED EMOTIONS

poetry *Pt* today

MIXED EMOTIONS

Edited by
Ruth Byars

First published in Great Britain in 1997 by Poetry Today, an imprint of Penhaligon Page Ltd, The Malthouse, Llangollen, Wales.

A Catalogue record for this book is available from the British Library.

ISBN 186226 0443

Typesetting and layout, Penhaligon Page Ltd, Wales.
Printed and bound by Forward Press Ltd, England

'Give me more love or more distaine;
The Torrid or the frozen Zone:
Bring equall ease unto my paine;
The temperate affords me none.
Either extreame, of love, or hate,
Is sweeter than a calme estate.'

(Thomas Carew, c1595 - 1640: 'Mediocritie in Love Rejected')

Foreword

When I selected the poems for *Mixed Emotions,* my aim was to incorporate traditional and contemporary poetry that would portray the 'mixed emotions' of love and relationships, both intimate and platonic I hope that I have achieved my goal and that you will enjoy reading this collection of poetry as much as I have.

The standard of poetry in *Mixed Emotions* was excellent and once again I had the unenviable task of having to choose three outright winners; a job made all the more difficult because of the wealth of talented writers who contributed to the book. However on this occasion the winners are:

P A McMenamin   Safe Return

Michelle Jeffery   Opposites

Richard Young   If you Should Learn to Me

My congratulations and thanks go to them and to all of you who have contributed to *Mixed Emotions.*

To

Kath + Eddie,

from,

Paul McMenamin

Contents

The Poems

Untitled

Grateful, I was, surely, for you
Given to me
And my life, that is mine was
Gratefully and faithfully all yours
to have and share

Fateful, I was, surely, were you
My heart given
To my wife, yet
Fate turned against my soul
Unrequited were you.

Hateful, I was, purely for you
Not forgiven,
For my strife that followed
Hating, left hollow, for you the thief
My heart did steal.

Jon Stanway

You

As you walked into my life,
My soul felt like an afterglow of the sun,
My heart was the colour of the inflamed Mars,
The countryside was still and motionless,
Flowers blooming with pureness and serenity,
I knew you would never go and leave,
Life was as total as perfection could get,
Illness fell about your soul,
I thought life would never fade away,
Until that sudden tragic day,
Now you are gone,
Life has reached its final conclusion,
Was it all a fantasy illusion?

Elizabeth Harknett (17)

The Lovers

She stares at the card
she has chosen
The Tarot man smiles
but the picture remains
the face still the same
Caught between
so uncertain
whose side will he turn
There's a young girl in rags
with her heart in his hands
and flowers
for her crown.
Woman stands so
compelling
crowned in rich beauty
and power of her craft
years of her art beckon
secret desires . . .
leading him on drawing him down
Reach for the flowers
or the flowers will fade.
The Tarot man smiles
his voice reassures . . .
the picture uncertain
pending the bow
The face
still the same.

Mary-Jamuna Charles

19

Notes

My name is Gail Knight. I am 36 years old, married with two children, Sarah aged 11 and Matthew aged 9.

I love to write poetry and find it very relaxing. some of my most creative moments have been during times of personal stress. writing can be very therapeutic.

This is the second poem I have had published.. The first was *The Witness* published last year in *Sands of Time.*

I would like to dedicate 'Revenge is Sweet' to my Nana, Hilda Wild, who I know loves to read my poetry.

Revenge is Sweet

The old man stood by the garden gate,
contemplating his sorry fate.
He'd stabbed his wife with a carving knife,
extinguishing every ounce of her life.

He looked out across the dusty road,
relieved at last to have shed his load.
The carving knife still in his grip.
He bit long and hard upon his lip.

He could always claim he was insane
after all those years of indescribable pain.
He tossed the knife upon the ground,
just missing Henry his trusty hound.

He ambled back across the path,
deciding he needed to take a bath.
It was here they found him lying cold,
looking oh so very old.

Heart attack, the doctor said.
He had been told to stay in bed.
Too much excitement for one day
and so now side by side they lay.

G Knight

We Grow Apart

Notes

I wrote this poem following
the break-up of a relation-
ship with a girlfriend to ex-
press my feelings about what
had happened.

Through writing poetry I am
able to give voice to my emo-
tions concerning significant
events in my life.

We grow apart - don't we
Not seeing each other
Now a difference
What's happening - just what?
Time goes on and distance constrains
We see each other but not what.
Say nothing with your words
No need to speak and then a question
It is to ask who you are
Past, present, future - are of no consequence
Anything of value - anything of being
We become strangers.

J Bayless

21

That's the Time I Think of You

I'm tired of waking
in the early hours of morning
waiting for a brighter dawning
to rest her head upon my pillow
but I'm a loner,
everything else is just dreaming.
Although the sun drifts in sometimes
there's usually a cloud in hot pursuit
to darken what ray I might have had
so I do not cling to sunshine
for tomorrow never knows.
The reaper's working late at night
his mournful seeds he sows and
loneliness is something
I do not need the most.
But when the sun comes
shines right through
That's the time I think of you.

J Carter

This poem was written for and is dedicated to Eve Kelly

Wishes for You

My wishes must warm you like a mother's embrace
Give you strength and courage for the world we face
Bring joy to your life, harbour you from mistakes
Above all they must allow you to write your own fate

I could wish you a fortune or a diamond ring
A life full of luxury, would it mean a thing?
In truth my dearest it's not all it seems
Have peace, love, happiness and all your childhood dreams

Mario Giovanni Bassi

Forbidden Love

Just one more touch, just one more kiss,
To feel the softness of your skin,
Oh, these are the things I so sadly miss,
Your loveliness so deep within.

To touch your hair to see you smile,
To share your worries and cradle your sorrow,
To be part of your life if just for a while,
And secretly wish that there'd be no tomorrow.

To walk back in time to when we were young,
To run through the corn without any fears,
Dance together when our songs were sung,
To dry your eyes when there were tears.

To sweep the snow on a cold winter morn,
Warm our hands by the burning log fire,
To wake to the chorus of birds at dawn,
To sing together with the church's choir.

But we were victims of class and society,
You a servant and me a Lord,
We did not want any notoriety,
Discovered as lovers, I could not afford.

J Foxley

Donna

Notes

This poem is simply a testimony of my love for Donna. Life with her is the best thing in the world; life without her is no life at all.

It is cold here now as it is cold everywhere
when my body is not with yours, my hand in your hair
of heaven's gold; my hands seem worthless now and old.

I wish that I could feel the sensual rise and fall
of you next to me in sleep
and hold your jewelled fingers to my lips and taste
your breath so soft and sweet;
but I strain to catch your murmurs as you slumber,
must close my eyes to see your ruffled sheet
the quilt pushed down dreamily at the corner.
What dreams, my love, bring you into morning
fresh as dew,
whilst I pass another sleepless night, my heart torn in two
by thoughts of pain and loss of life without you?

Like partners in a seance, apart yet together -
would that I could make my feelings known across the ether
to be caught, a fragile butterfly, by you and pinned
onto a board forever, untouched by sin
and never changing, preserved beneath a bell-jar from decay -
would that things could be this way
on a solitary night in
with only memory to keep me warm and safe,
memory of your smiling mouth and lovely upturned face.

Mark Lewis

25

Notes

Aged 48, I am married with two daughters, live in Swindon town centre and work for the Local Authority.

I began writing verses in Summer 1995, and in January 1996 submitted a combination of three verses to the International Society of Poets who were running monthly competitions. It appeared in their anthology *The Other side of the Mirror* published in August 1996.

Since then I have continued to enter competitions and my poems have been published by The Poetry Guild, Poetry in Print, Poetry Today and Forward Press. One of my earlier pieces also received an Award of Excellence.

Writing poetry enables me to express thoughts and feelings of anxiety, frustration, helplessness, sadness, joy et cetera but also allows me to acknowledge changes in the world around us.

I enjoy reading fantasy novels, crosswords, needlecraft, music, and entering competitions.

Love

Love can make you happy
it can also make you sad,
Love can make you angry
and can also drive you mad.
The little things you say and do
are so wrong in his eyes,
Being slow to praise
but quick to criticise.

If you try to help him
you just get in the way,
But when you try to leave
he's begging you to stay.
It's very hard to please him
no matter how you try,
And though he stole your heart
you often wonder why.

Sometimes it gets confusing
not knowing what to do,
As with a smile and a hug
he's making up to you.
Knowing you'll forgive him
as so many times before,
A gentle kiss will make you melt
in his arms once more.

G Gallo

Notes

This poem was written in retrospect to my first true love my first everything. Back then I was too inexperienced to deal with the problems that arose especially when you are just grasping and understanding love and the courtship game. Insecurity was all to prevalent in my early teens and my failings were ones of nonecommunication. The only way I felt comfortable showing my feelings was through my poems. It was all too easy to call it a day; a case of 'You can't live with her, you can't live without her'. But when you feel trapped and backed into a corner you either come out fighting or give up and get beaten. Sometimes the learning process can be a right bitch. In love you're either a winner or a loser, so far I seem to have become a winner from losing. But who knows what the future holds for me, now I have experience on my side?

The Last Days of Pompeii - The Beginning of the End?

There is an aching in my heart,
When we are apart,
But when we're together
Down comes the bad weather;
The storms brew,
Words are said,
Which has the impact of lightning in my head.

Things are starting to become sour,
Is this the beginning of our last hour?
Is it time to pack up my bags and go?
Or just stay and deceive people
With what they don't already know?

The road has been laid,
For the mistakes I have made,
The signs have already been set,
For the end of the road, I'll bet!

So once again my options are limited,
As to what to do,
Do I abandon the sinking ship,
Or stand the test?
In my mind neither is easy to digest.

Can it survive a week, a month
Come what may,
Or is it just 'The last days of Pompeii?'

Paul Doody

Safe Return

In our room at the top of our house is our bed, on the floor at the end lie
your shoes.
And I remember that when you first went away, I stared at them whilst
waiting for news.
In the hall by the door is the table of oak, the one which you made in a day.
On the table the phone sits alone quietly and it's not rung since you've been
away.

There's a gate at the end of the path to our house, the gate where you
kissed me goodbye.
and I watched you march off in your uniform and I hoped God would not
let you die.
In the belly upon which you lay your sweet head, a life is starting to form.
And I hope you'll be home from that far foreign shore before our baby is
born.

They say that the best news is no news at all, if that's so, then I'm doing
well.
But I wish I could know that you have survived for I know that a war is
like hell.
If love can protect you, then here in my heart, is a shield that will help you
to live.
And if God exists then he's heard me pray and you'll be back for I've more
love to give.

P A McMenamin

Amateur Love Poetry

She stood in utmost splendour and glory
As chaste as the morning dew
Her black hair reflecting upon pale flesh
Unblemished and true
She turned and held out her arms
As I floated unto her womb
There we did embrace in our bower of bliss
Our castle joyous did we then live
Yet in our sin were we chaste
Nothing unnatural in our embrace
Above the harmonic spheres we danced
They sang in tune with our romance

We mingled and entwined souls became one
My blood did flow unto her heart
Our life-liquids mingled in the flow of love
Though I do praise her body and looks
Her charms and treasures that I took
Will never be read in this here book
For though I write of love and of blood
Of procreation throughout all seasons
I cannot express in verse the way I feel
For I am no Shakespeare, Sidney or Donne
Spenser is beyond me despite all I have done
Yet here, do I praise my love.

John Heginbotham

Notes

I would like to dedicate this poem to my dear son Michael, who sadly died six years ago.

Michael has left an empty space in my heart that no one else could fill. Although he suffered for many years, his love and loyalty for me and his brothers and sisters never failed to amaze me. He has left us with many loving memories one of them was his warm hearted nature which will be with Gill, Debbie, Peter, Paul, and Sarah forever. I know their love for their brother grows, alongside those precious memories of our Michael, he will be in our hearts and thoughts through to eternity, as true love never dies.

Love

Love, can conquer, all the despair
many troubles, are halved, if shared.
Love is unselfish, priceless, so free
it is something to feel, often to see.

Love is like food, feeding the brain,
although eating, and loving
of course, are not the same,
love nourishes, from deep within.

Love, or to be loved, unconditionally
provides the stepping stones of life, to care,
a stone may turn, or suffer inwardly,
but with empathy, once more,
with love to share.

Sally Nolan

The Pebble's Journey

He was a pebble: Small, blanched and flat -
Peppered,
Nondescript,
Drawn this way, sent that;
Swathed by the grasping tide . . .
Worked to something smooth . . .
Deluged,
And plied.
Where is his strength? He's overpowered.
Day by day, he is devoured.

She was a fierce ocean,
A rolling wave,
Sweeping devotion -
To a shallow grave.
She was relentless, determined.
She would not yield:
But he had a heart of stone -
With its might to wield.
He resisted. He anchored. She had to learn
That this small pebble had lost his turn.

She frothed, harsh and frenzied,
Then left with an angry roar.

The pebble joined his friends
On a golden shore.

Dawn Carol

31

The Romany

A lilting lament o'er the heathland by a girl, pretty and young,
Dog at her heels on the pathway, hair a'glint in the sun.
True and clear in the evening air, a song as old as time,
Wearing a dress of faded blue, her curly hair like tawny wine.
With ease she walked with a long stride, her body straight and fine,
Over the moor our paths were crossed, as we neared her eyes met mine,
Still with a step to match her song unhurried she passed me by,
I doffed my cap and bade 'Good evening,' such was her beauty for which
                                                                    men die.

I watched the distance between us growing wider with each stride,
She was walking towards the village, head held high, a natural pride.
I knew where she was heading, an encampment one mile further on
With the gypsies, hard working and restless, the men jealous and strong.
I often saw her from then on, always singing as she walked,
At last, one evening I bade her well and she stopped to talk.
A young man has his fancy, he knows when he is smitten,
No snobbery in my character, by the gypsy's love bug I am bitten.
This Romany a lovely girl, spent many hours with me
Talking and walking with her dog, o'er the moorland, wild and free.
When twilight came and campfires lit, I bade the lass 'Goodnight,'
Nodding to the elders, I doffed my cap and walked by in the night.
Alas, when next I waited at our usual trysting place
In vain, my eyes searched o'er the moor, to see her lovely face,
Her dainty figure, striding through the trodden heath,
Night descended, I walked the moor, sad, with leaden feet
To the village, to the camp, and there to my dismay
The campsite, cleared and empty, they had gone that very day.
Now a broken-hearted youth, cursed gypsy elders for their spite
Must learn to live without the love, he thought he had for life.

Patti Ryall

32

Notes

Jeanette Clinton was born 15th November 1955 in London. She has been married since 1986 to Michael and has two daughters, Sarah Louise and Wendy Jane. She is a housewife and lives in Preetz, which is in Schleswig-Holstein, Germany (approximately 50 miles from the Danish border).

She has had four poems published in separate anthologies and was in the final of the 1996 International Open Poetry Contest.

Her hobbies are writing, music, nature and her family. She started writing poetry at the age of 15, as a means to express herself and has written poems ever since. Her inspirations are gained by feelings or events of the moment.

Because I Love You

Give me your hand and I'll show you the way.
Give me your smile to brighten my day.
Give me your heart and you will see,
I'll give you my love for eternity.

Give me your time, precious moments to share.
Give me your body, to love and care.
Give me your soul to protect within me, and
I'll give you my life - an eternity.

Give me your sorrows, your joy, your pain.
Give me a chance, just let me explain.
Give me your patience, your open heart, and
I'll give you a moment of love, a start.

Give me your time, so I can talk with you.
Give me your doubts about life as two.
Give me your trust, hear the words I say, and
I'll give you the meaning of each new day.

Give me your arms to hold me tight.
Give me your breath to warm my night.
Give me your lips to taste the time
I gave you my love within this rhyme.

Give me an hour of your hectic day.
Give me a look, in that special way.
Give me your voice, to hear you say my name, and
I'll give you a moment to think again.

But all this you gave me so long ago.
All these moments, and now I know,
I never gave you the chance to say
The words I speak now, each and every day.

I believed your feelings were not true,
Not as the feelings I felt for you.
It was I, not you, that walked away.
Turn back the clock, give me back that day.

But I am glad I could share with you
A few precious hours, kind and true.
For the words we spoke, and words untold,
are mine alone, to treasure and hold.

I wish you love, a feeling so deep.
I wish you joy, moments to keep.
I wish you happiness along the way,
and I wish you everything I felt, for you, that day.

Jeanette Clinton

33

Inamorato

Notes

'Peri', me!
Sweet inspirational you!.

I don't just love you,
I live you.
I wake with you on my mind
And go to sleep the same way.
During the day you cross my mind
And I smile.
In a store,
On the street,
People must think me crazy sometimes.
What makes me smile?
The look you cast my way
When you think no one is looking.
Your touch when we pass,
Your goodnight kiss,
The joke that's just between us.

You walk in a room.
It may be filled with people
I see only you.
The sound of your voice
Makes my heart sing.
Someone mentions your name,
Oh! sweet joy.
I could go on and on.
I guess, it's that I'm so in love.
With everything that makes you my life.

Kay Reynolds

My Morning Thoughts

Consumed by the famous fires of passion,
I dare to touch your untouchable skin,
So far out of reach are you,
An illusion, a prize I cannot win.

Love to me is my only aim,
Not lustful longing in such a hurried way,
I can't stop my thoughts telling me,
I only have you for a day.

It all seems so tender it all seems so right,
I only want your warmth and arms around me,
Not screaming orgasms into the night,
I'm happy to kiss you until the dawn,
I've been waiting so long,
In one hour I will have to mourn, something that I shouldn't have done.

You're someone else's prize,
You look into someone else's eyes,
I want to be her in the blink of an eye,
If I was would I listen to you lie.

Louise Stocker

Beauty

In the twinkle of an eye,
Beauty sparkles with a smile,
Like diamonds in the sky,
Stars of the heavenly night,
Beauty is my high,
My guidance, my light.

Beauty is the creation,
For every vibration.
Like the scent of symphony,
When every rose is harmony,
Like every season, a melody.

Beauty is a kiss,
The mother of eternal bliss.
Like the shades of sunset,
When colours of peace are met,
These visions of beauty, I'll never forget.

Rivers of dreams,
Through golden streams,
This flow of energy,
This grace of beauty,
Like dolphins in the ocean blue,
This dance of beauty,
Is me and you.

Sutharman Kanagarajah

A Bitter Love

Your love is like a locked door,
To which I've not the key.
The situation makes me deplore,
Why you will not love me.

Inside that door is a joy,
Which I will never find.
You treat my heart like a toy,
You manipulate my mind.

My frustrated passions turn to hate,
The love I bore has gone.
I once thought you were my fate;
Now it's time to move on.

C Johnson

Notes

The author was born in Soli-
hull, West Midlands in 1970
to parents Keith and Eileen
Maling.

Other publications include
Elegy of the Damned in *Be-
tween a Laugh and a Tear* by
The International Society of
Poets (1966) which won the
Editor's Choice Award. *Unti-
tled* in *Sands of Time* by Po-
etry Today (1996) '*Ode to
Poetic Stimuli* in *Light of the
World* by The International
Library of Poetry (1997)
Editor's Choice Award.

'*Love Pending*' is taken from
the uncompleted anthology of
Poetry entitled *Elegies of the
Damned,* a collection of po-
etry that comes straight from
the heart of the damned soul.
This collection was due for
completion this year. How-
ever as unpredictable as the
heart so to is that which it
exudes, for now it issues
forth an unexpected third
phase of poetry for which I
am eternally grateful for po-
etry really has become the
amaranth of my heart.

Love Pending

Oh to be another
To live a lover's dream
I pray my life forever transpose
With what has never been

Oh to feel the passion
Of love's attraction blind
To spur the souls sweet opium flow
(The elixir of halcyon mind)

To find the hidden secret
For which I covet evermore
The elusive covert vestibule:
The pathway lovers traverse unsure

Oh if fate awaits me
Then Nemesis hear my pleas implore
As absence grows I pray disclose
An end to days lovelorn.

Lee Martin Maling

Him!

Do you think sometimes,
When you look at his face.
You'd like to smack him
Once with a mace?

Don't you think that
He gets on your nerves,
And one day he'll get
What he deserves?

You've been together
For a long time now.
Go on, take a swing
And hit him now.

But then again, sometimes
He can be really sweet.
Even when he suffers
From sweaty feet?

He knows you better
Than you know yourself.
For without him,
You'd be on the shelf.

I suppose you fit together
Like a hand in a glove.
I think you may have forgotten
The thing that is love.

So look at him
And smile again.
He's what you could call
Your only best friend.

Gaynor Cowell .

A Prayer of Love

Cherish me - is all I ask you
        as the greatest gift in shower,
To give your love free and as true
        as the perfume of a flower.

Hold me - against in your heart's frame
        with all tenderness in fold,
Keep me safe from a world in shame
        with its grasping evil hold.

Caress me - as though a petal
        of the rarest satin plush,
With the corolla and sepal
        in the smoothest gentle blush.

Love me - with a passion that burns
        like the hottest sun in shine,
That ever warms my heart which learns
        to hasten with yours in twine.

Leave me - never that I would die
        at the void to make bereft,
My soul which is all yours in life
        entwined with you in love's theft.

To be beside - is the desire
        fanning in my heart as led,
By the bright flame of you on fire
        with the love you gave and pled.

Aileen Hopkins

She Always Sang

Notes

I am aged fifty five, married with seven children and living in Kent. I am an English teacher.

She always sang - she sang around the house
And in her morning bath - she sang in shops
And as she drove the car - but then she married
And within a year the singing stopped.

Her husband, if not kind, was not unkind -
It was not what he said but what he did not
Say - what he did but what he failed
To do - what he remembered but forgot -

What - quite simply - he was not. For thirty
Years she lived a life of songless grief
And when he died she did not cry but in
Her bath she sang once more for sheer relief.

Angela Hall

Notes

This will be my third poem
published by Poetry Today
and I thank them for publish-
ing my work.

In Good Time

My head is full
My heart is empty
My eyes see you
My ears hear nothing

Your picture on my wall
Your picture in my head
Your face hovers above me
When I'm in bed
The night you left weighs
heavily on my mind
I see you all the time
sometime I wish I was blind.
I see your face when I lay awake at night
I see your face when I turn out my light:
I read a book but you're still in my head
I see your face when I get out of bed.
I was there for you when you needed me
Why did you leave why must that be?
I loved you with all my heart;
Why must we be apart?
Time will be the antidote for love sickness.

Daniel Proctor

Notes

I am a 21 year old student nurse at St Bart's Hospital, in London. I have been writing poetry for several years. About Love is a poem that I wrote in an attempt to comprehend a complex emotion that no man has yet been able to truly understand.

Poetry is often an individual and subjective response to experiences through life. This poem holds a special place in my heart for its meaning to me.

Dedicated to my stepfather, Jim.

About Love

I used to look towards the heavens . . .
The stars, the moon: a cosmic world.
I used to wonder if there could ever be
A place for me sometime, somewhere.

No more do I have to roam,
Searching for my part to play.
I am no longer lost, but home,
Together, here, with you.

You have given me love . . .
Love, which as a tree,
Grows and blossoms as the years pass by
And reaches out towards the sky . . .

Eternity.

Georgina Hindley

My Hurt for You

To touch your hand,
To comb your hair,
To laugh with you,
To hold you near,
To hear your voice,
To squeeze you tight,
To kiss your cheek,
To wish 'Goodnight,'
I miss you so,
You made my world, my life,
In parting now, I feel death's knife,
Not the knife to kill, but the pain of death,
But I'll love you still, deep with every breath.

Sarah Hinton

Notes

I was born on the 3rd February 1938 in Wilmslow, Cheshire. I trod the boards in repertory after leaving school at sixteen.

After training as a nurse and midwife, I worked for two years in America, in the Kentucky Mountains, with the Frontier Nursing Service, travelling to visit patients by jeep or on horseback. Whilst in the States, a friend and I toured 10,000 miles around the National Parks in a hearse called 'Bu-Bu' (but that is another story).

Most of my nursing career has been spent in caring for very frail elderly people. For twenty years I was Officer-in-Charge of a County Council Elderly Person's Home, in Loughborough. I took early retirement and now live in Mundesley. Our house looks out upon the sea.

My husband, George and I, live with Tess, the dog and Tibby and Tilly the cats. Our son still lives in Loughborough but visits often.

I think I have always written poems and stories. I care very much about animals and often write poems to support various causes, several of which have been published.

Did You Love Me?

Oh how I loved you, all those years ago.
Loved you with the kind of love I'd never thought to know.
A love which recreated me, enslaved, yet set me free
But you, my dear and only love, did you, in truth, love me?

You said you did, as you held me tight
Said our love was good and fine and right.
Apart from me you felt bereft,
You hated to leave, but you always left.

Fragile as a gossamer web, strong as tempered steel,
The stuff of dreams and fairy tales suddenly made real.
I loved you with elation, I loved you with despair
With hope and fear and joy and pain, blasphemy and prayer.
Through light and dark, in fair and foul, in misery and glee
But you, my dear and only love, did you, in truth, love me?

You said you did, wished you were free
A little while . . . just wait and see.
For our love was strong 'twould root and grow.
Just one more kiss and you had to go.

Alas, time's river carried us along our different ways
And filled our lives with this and that, lost us in a maze
Of being there and doing things and functioning on cue.
But always when my world stood still, my love I thought of you

Now the years are gone, but the memories stay
I loved you then as I do today.
Though you tore my heart I darned the tear
My love was constant, always there.
And that's enough . . . well, it has to be
For I'll never know if you loved me.

Tricia Sturgeon

My Lady in Red

A vision of colour so vividly etched
Deep into mind and heart
The bodice buttoned to neck to waist
Enclosing that warm loving heart

The sleeves that reach to the curves
Of those arms so loving and inviting
Leading down to those long slender fingers
Which wears my ring so openly and lovingly

The gathered waist so slimly covered
Where on times my arms have rested
Whilst walking so lovingly through
The fields so happiness so tested

The flowing skirt so widely spread
As wide and deep as my love for you
Long and bright just as the memories
So loving shared by me and you

Above that colour, a head of golden hair
With a face of beauty unbounded
Hazel eyes and pink small ripe lips
The ones I love to kiss on their very tips

The face that shows the love
And passion to for only one to read
A smile that is more beautiful
Than roses in their bed
And more warmth than the sun's rays
That's my lady in red

John Bower

Untitled

Hold me gently for I might break
Wrap strong arms about me
Soothe my soul, mend my heart -
Don't worry, I won't love you, I can't -
I just need someone to take away the pain
Wash away the sadness, put a bandage on the shame
Perhaps I'm wrong to use you -
But my loss is just so great
Heal me, hold me, care for me,
Perhaps it's not too late . . .

Virginia Thomas

Dead Rose Not Breathing

I look at the wilted rose in the vase
and think it means the end of love
not breathing, not talking, just thinking
of the days when we never had worries
when we never thought twice
just laughing and joking and talking
but all of that is over
there is no proof that it happened at all
except the photo that sits on the table
and the dead rose that says it all

Rebecca Jones

Notes

My name is Lucy Reading. I am 18 years old and I live in Newport, south Wales.

this is my third published poem.

Please was written in 1995 and is about my boyfriend of two years, Keeran. Although I loved him very much his sarcastic 'wit' and questionable actions would make me feel insecure and unhappy. We split up April 1997.

Please

You tell me I'm perfect in your eyes:
I'm beautiful - your prize,
Yet you criticise.
Your insults sometimes cut so deep
I feel them bleeding, even when I sleep.
They hurt me
degrade me.
You make me cry
whilst your lovely face stays dry.
No tears from you I see,
That's because you are free, to be.
And yet you promise you tried
not to crush my precious pride.
You lied.

Lucy Reading

Watchful Moon

Sometimes in the midst of winter
when the skies are dark and grey,
I long for the warmth of that summer's night
when in my loved one's arms I lay.

The sound of distant music,
the lull of a romantic tune,
we pledged our love forever
with a kiss under a watchful moon.

The balmy air wrapped round us,
there was no rush, though it was quite late,
all we wanted was to be together
and that night we sealed our fate.

Our parents rallied round us
though they felt we were too young,
but we knew this was forever,
true living had just begun.

The years that followed after
were full of laughter and love,
our lives, never tinted with sadness,
had surely been blessed by one above.

Now the children have grown and left us,
that part was over way too soon,
but I'll never forget how it started -
long ago, under a watchful moon.

Lesley Wright

After 24 Years

Yesterday you spoke, and I found you boring,
Last night I woke, and you were snoring,
But I used to listen to every word you said,
And you used to love me enough, I would sleep like the dead.

You came home yesterday, and said hello to my friend,
You didn't kiss my cheek, you didn't even pretend,
No, you don't bring me flowers, or make me laugh anymore,
But I still listen for your car, still wait for your key in the door.

You were late one day, not very long ago,
You'd had an accident they'd said - and God I loved you so!
I drove to where you were, I screamed your name out loud,
I pushed past official people, I parted ghoulish crowd,
And there you were, bright blanket, matching bleeding face,
Shocked eyes staring, arm outstretched for my embrace.

You were brave then, stupid my love, but brave,
You still went to work the next day, with never a backward wave,
And I swore I would be kinder, calmer, letting you know I still cared,
But our work and our days took over, and still how little we shared.

Last week your arm crept round my waist, caressing and insisting,
I found myself enjoying it, responding, not resisting,
And if passion can flare in the hush of the night,
Is our love still there, and everything all right?

So next year is the big one - a medal for us two,
And somehow our love has survived, despite what we've been through,
Or maybe it is something else, that will see us through to the end,
But if it's not love darling, then please let us pretend.

Thérèse Fisher

Walk on Water

I'll come to you
Across time zones and borders
I'll be with you
Across rivers and oceans
I'll think of you
Across days and weeks
I'll write to you
Send postcards and letters
I'll come to you
With words of tenderness
I'll be with you
With encouragement and coffee
I'll down tools and drive anywhere
To spend a moment with you
I'll think of you
My mind will spin dizzily
It will transport me to even attempt
To walk on water.

Sam Goodman

Love's Gift

They lay before the log fire,
Kissing and caressing,
Having satisfied desire,
Giving, not suppressing,
They lay thinking, as lovers do,
About the things that they both knew,
That whatever life may give them,
Or perhaps may take away,
This part of life was always theirs,
Not just something for today,
Love is the greatest gift that we can give,
Or that we may receive,
And however long our lives may be,
I know that I believe,
That love lives on forever,
It is the greatest force we know,
That somewhere in the spirit world,
That love will grow and grow,
In the massive scheme of things,
Two lovers may seem small,
But they both have eternal love,
The greatest gift of all.

Barrie Strong

Notes

My husband has always had a
keen interest in North Ameri-
can History and one day
whilst I was in his office I
noticed a Bronze bust of Red
Indian Chief. Gazing at this
proud figure of a man gave
me the inspiration to write
Echoes in the Dark.

*I dedicate this poem to my
husband Pete who has always
encouraged me with my po-
etry.*

Echoes in the Dark

Happy with the silence
and now the dust is stirred
Like a ghost he has returned
looking so disturbed

The tribe were dancing in the dark
- horses running wild.
As fate led me to his pointed face
amidst the striking crowd.

Like a bird looking on its prey
wearing beads of different shades.
As he gives a glance of pride,
his strong black hair flows
- as he walks each stride.

Enchantingly moving swiftly round and round
reaching up then touching ground
his hand to his mouth making talking sound.

Our eyes met
we walked away
- but just in time
I realised then
I'd but dreamt again

Caroline Holder

God's Greetest Gift

Notes

I am 28 years old. I live in Bathampton near Bath and poetry has always been one of my great many hobbies which I take heart from

Elegant, graceful, her beauty and disguise
Passionate and loving her crystal blue eyes.
Fragile, tender, her body and touch
Gifted further by her intimidating kiss.

Comforting and caring while in her arms
Overwhelming the power of her charms
Stunning, outstanding, the clothes she wears
Shiny and sparkly her clean long hair.

All features she possesses night and day,
Leaving her man helpless, taking his breath away,
Admirable, talented all around,
Encouraged by her loveable ways.

Nothing compares to the determination she shows
Her dignity, pride and respect within,
Reasons why she should be loved more
She's a winner for me by a long long score.

Jaul James Old

Love

How does love start,
When does love end,
Even though I am just a friend,
Is it a sin when it is within,
Always knowing, but never showing,
On a face there is grace,
Deep down there is a frown,
Tears, pain and sorrows,
For there won't be many more tomorrows,
Going, going, gone
Like something to be sold,
Is it a soul! Never,
For God's grace will walk
        Forever.

A L Harper

A Moment, our Child

Notes

Maybe I'm an old romantic; I don't know! The idea for this poem came to me when I was alone thinking about families and loved ones, and a possible future with children of my own.

Your monogamous hand reaches to my body,
Laying gently there at peace with your silence.
Another reaches and holds my jaw and cheek,
A hold so strong, never allowed to be weak.
So innocently pure,
No innocence taken.
Still there when we awaken.
Our act of loving made in the scented light,
Taken into warm pastures we cannot fight.
We wake, we smile, we loved awhile.
We held each other within that smile full of the knowing
We will have our child.
Our child made from love.

Ciaran Rafferty

My Secret Love

Dear are the moments when to my inner eye I turn and I am free
Passion and you my dear like some old friend
Steal in to keep me company
And once again your smiling eyes beguile me
Then the soft warm glow and the racing heartbeats start
And I feel the tightening of the throat
And the burning hand that touches at my heart

Why do you captivate me so
What is your secret yet alas
Where were you when I searched
Or was our meeting not meant to pass
Until another moment in time

Your eyes are open wide no fear in them I see
All I see is love and the reflection of me
I try to look more deeply as if by doing so
I could read your very soul
And I can see the unspoken love that from your eyes glow
And I echo the unspoken words 'I love you so'

Together in my private world
Where everything is perfect and everywhere is peace
I put my arms around you and hold you close
Trying to find the antidote
So this ache in my heart will cease
But my love before you slip away
Into the other world where we are not free
I'll hold you one more time close to me and say
I'll try to understand that our love cannot be
Unless! In the book of life
Our names are entwined and blessed from above
But if they are not you'll always be
'My Secret Love'

Cindy Lansdell

Notes

Born into a large family in New Zealand in 1950, married at 19 to a beautiful 20 year old. Four children arrived to fulfil our dreams. I was widowed in 1988 and since then I have watched our children grow into delightful caring beings all in their own right.

Like my children I have also grown to know and understand who I am. Not just as a mother, the baby sister or even the daughter, but just me - Shona Brown.

The poem *Let Us* is one of the many written in reflection of what I needed in my life.' Simplicity'. Free from those who tried to make a square peg fit into a round hole; only to find out it was not others as much as it was myself.

I dedicate this poem to my mother and to the memory of my father who taught me the importance of being just me.

Let Us

Let us think
in quiet moments.
Let us think
with open souls.
Let us think about tomorrow.
Let us think.
Let us think.

Let us speak
but not in riddles.
Let us speak
with open minds.
Let us speak with honest feelings.
Let us speak.
Let us speak.

Let us sing
but not in sadness.
Let us sing
with loving words.
Let us sing in joyful chorus.
Let us sing.
Let us sing.

S Brown

First Kiss

It wasn't that special,
I remember.
In fact, I recall it with positive distaste.
It was an invasion of my privacy -
An entry into my person.
How dare he assume it so easily?
Yes, it was an unpleasant thing
But somehow addictive.
My return for more surprised me,
And I grew to enjoy;
To want; to need;
Until the kiss was never enough.

Clare King

I Remember You

Notes

The author is married with two children and lives in Oxfordshire.

I see you often now,
Bouncing through the place that we call memory,
Mysteriously hidden in the grey cells of the brain,
I see your enthusiasm for life,
Your love, your great big sloppy kisses,
I see your plans and your dreams,
I feel the grass beneath your bare feet,
The muddy wet water as you paddle in a stream,
I see the small pink grass peas blooming just for you,
I hear the birds and see the cows pass by,
I climb the gates and chase the errant lambs,
I fall from the swing and slide in the cow muck with you,
I run with you across the dark dark yard,
Fleeing from the terrors of the darkness.
You would like the small reincarnation that I live with now,
Just like you,
Except he is a boy,
The masculine in both that made you a tomboy,
The feminine in both that makes him unusually sensitive.
But sometimes when I see you
You do not laugh.
You scream and accuse me,
What did I do with your life, your hopes, your dreams?
I have betrayed them all,
I am your future and I have destroyed you.

Selina Robertson

Notes

I started writing poems whilst at school and this is now my second to be published, which I'm very pleased about. I enjoy writing for my own pleasure, but I am constantly trying to improve, whilst maintaining my own individual style.

People still comment on how sombre my poems are, and although I've been told they are good, not everyone understands them. Something I respect as poetry is very personal and different to everyone.

since I had my first poem published I have felt more confident about letting other people read them and have discovered that some of them also write.

This poem as with my last one is not written about my feelings or a personal experience, it merely tries to capture an awareness of the many elements of love that we might feel, and our need for someone special - something we can all relate to. It is also about striving to reach a balance between physical and emotional feelings.

I still live at home with my parents and I work with children, but I would also like to try and further develop my writing skills.

Fool's Dream

Passionate embraces,
fires lit, within
a soul in need
of warmth.
A need to cherish,
and hold, to care.
With meaning
from both.
Physical ecstasy of
a promise made,
late at night.
Two bodies swaying,
reaching out with
unspoken words.
Capturing the feelings
too long known,
but too scared
to acknowledge.
Like ashes
scattered, confusion
beats logic, with
a desire too
strong to ignore,
but lost in the
essence of a
time and situation,
so right, but so wrong.

Karen Collisson

The Windows to the Soul

Notes

I have been writing for some time. I write mostly poems which take about 15 seconds to write because it's usually in a moment of inspiration. sometimes I write everyday and then I write nothing for weeks, it depends on whether I have anything to say. There was no particular inspiration for this poem except that I hope one day I will feel like that about somebody.

You have a hold over me,
Something draws me to you:
A voice,
Dwelling somewhere deep inside my mind.
I don't understand you,
Yet you stir feelings in me that I can't explain.
You're a part of me,
You're inside my thoughts, you're everywhere,
At the very soul of my existence,
But I don't know that you're the voice,
Crying out in the darkness,
You're the voice that makes my world spin so fast.
You've got me,
Right where you want me,
A sacrifice on your altar,
I know you and what it is you want.
You want it,
Come and get it,
Find me, your voice isn't enough,
I have to see your soul when you talk.
Now you're here,
Even though you're miles away.
I can see your eyes, staring at me so hard,
A gaze that goes right through me.
That's when I know.

Erica Jones

Brief Eclipse

You were to me a sun-splashed dance on a summer's day,
So living, yet never loving . . .
Your smile seemed to hold promises of more intimate kisses
        But what was I to know in my foolish youth?

Now you seem little more than a faded print
in a locked, dusty drawer . . .
to be taken out . . . very occasionally . . . and smiled at
        now the tears have gone

No bitterness, as you lived only for you
I was a cloud on your horizon, depressing your breeze through life.
        You danced on though - oh how you danced!
Taking my breath away
                with each
                        ruthless
                                step

Yet,
        I,
                loved you

My mind no longer wants to remember our eclipse,
Me, the sad, solitary disc, alone with the stars . . .
        You never saw that I shone too . . .
You burnt so brightly, with such energy, such power
        I had no choice but to surrender.

You captured my heart in your rays.
It is funny to think that now
                I
                feel
                        nothing.

Sarah Bird

64

How Softly How Silently

Notes

Being a devout Roman Catholic I am inspired by the apparitions of the Holy Mother of God who has been appearing with most frequency especially in the 20th Century, her message is of one unconditional love and forgiveness to all humanity who she appears to irrespective of colour, creed, or nationality. She calls the world to repentance, and ending of all hostilities between nations and an increased spiritual awareness.

To Her I Dedicate my poem 'How Softly How Silently' Especially 'Our Lady of Medjugorje'

I hope you enjoy my finished work.

Scarlet shadows
Swift as they linger
As I climb
The silver mountain
Enchanted but driven
For the one I seek
See how she comes
Softly, softly, softly
To hear her voice
For love is like
The wild wind
As I call
Whispering how quietly

As moonbeams shimmer
Upon a cloud
Young girls come dancing
Singing songs
For the one I love
For the one I love
How softly
How silently
She came
As she comes to me
To catch eternity
Eternity
Here and now
Here and now

Amen

C D McIntosh

Untitled Sonnet

Notes

A teacher in my early thirties, I have been writing poetry, infrequently like most people, since my mid-teens. Teenage angst developing into thirty-something angst.

At the time of writing I found the description of the sonnet form useful - even if it does lead to 'wintery' in order to create that elusive tenth syllable.

I have no intention of writing any more sonnets.

You are my compass in love's sweet voyage,
aiding direction by the golden shine
which, pouring from your heavenly vantage,
gives light to the rugged path which is mine.
And when in this black void my path is lost,
no future glimpses can I see before
me, the gentle breeze you are blows the dust
from my eyes: such disclosure is too raw.
Wintery darkness descends upon this
glorious summer which is now buried
in you. Cold the fire, which burning is
a beacon for the love now lost and dead.
    The path to you is o'ergrown and hidden,
    the lodestone stolen, the thief forgiven.

Tom Jackson

Cathartic Cuisine

Notes

This piece was written as a reaction to the one-sided breakdown of a relationship.

She was a first-love and the fallout was protracted and very bitter.

Cynicism seemed like such a welcoming womb at the time.

There's something about carrion love -
Compulsion and the stench.
Like a vulture raping a dead dove,
And wondering where all the enthusiasm went.

Once - warm states of flesh are faded -
Skin stiffens to the touch.
Table-manners, uniquely jaded,
For the rupture of rapport's bled a little too much.

Feelings can't connect; gut gets riled -
Still force - feeds on this mess.
Like a helpless, malevolent child,
Unable to wean from the withering breast.

Gorge on a rotting relationship:
In the wake of meet, a legacy
Of poisoned meat and spoiled emotion - trips

Decorum is, with a tasteless feast:
To carve our losses and lick all wounds,
Is true manner of the beast

No sanctuary in gluttony:
Only miserable, picked - clean bones.
And no appetite to carry on love.

Andy Smith

Song

Take me and hold me close in your arms
and sing me a song that tells of my charms
and promise to keep me safe from all harm
and lover be good to me.
Take me and hold me so tight I can't breathe
and tell me the lie that you'll never leave
and tell it so well that I will believe
that lover you're good for me.
And when you must leave then do it with style
and make me believe you'll be back in a while
and let me live on with my dream in denial
yes lover be good to me.

Clive Johnson

Notes

Originally born in England in 1964, I have been in Aberdeen since 12 years of age. I live alone with my young son, Robbie, who inspires many things; not all of them poetic.

Following the birth of my son and the breakdown of my marriage, I resigned myself to single parenthood, with all its merits and hardships. After giving Robbie the best foundation for life that I could, he entered into the education system at age five, leaving me free to further my education. After five years of intermittent study and a lot of hard graft, in 1997, in the third year of a BA in Applied social Studies with Diploma in Social Work.

My poetry writing has developed gradually over the years, inspired by the people and situations that influence my life.

Silent Meeting

She sensed an external presence;
Someone focusing on she.
Simply standing watching,
the stranger on the periphery.

Friends loud and joyous;
she did accompany
Several, lively fun filled hours.
The gentleman's attention she inherited with glee.
Unspoken advances; from which neither cowers.

The man remains silent and still.
Of movement toward her, he shows no degree.
She's aware of the symmetrical couples;
the dance floor that they fill.
Tonight she decides,
alone, she will not be.

Overcome by a wave of abandon
she approaches the man by the bar.
Gently persuading,
his hand held in hers,
she leads him on to the floor.

Their bodies come together.
The music they ignore.
Kisses without introduction.
Uncharacteristically for her
with the man,
she heads for the door.

Nice Mickey

Notes

At present, I live in Truro, Cornwall, in a complex for the older person (I am the manager). I have worked with the elderly for about 13 years, which I see as my vocation.

Whenever was written for my partner of seven years when he was going through a difficult time in his life.

I have had about 10 poems published to date, mainly in anthologies with other poets. My ambition is to have a small book of my own poems published, in the hope that people who read them can either be helped, or gain comfort, by knowing that they are not unique in their suffering, whether in love or life.

Whenever

Whenever you need me
I will always be there
Whenever you want me
Just give me a stare
Whenever I see you
With love in your eyes
I am drawn like a magnet
Forget all your lies
Your touch gives me shivers
I feel lost in your arms
The world stops existing
I see only your charms
A mist seems to surround us
A haze vibrant and blue
Trance like and drugged
Magical feeling, being with you
Whenever the parting
I will always be there
When I think of you
I will always know you care
Whenever the tears be-dim my eyes
I will be happy I knew you
So deep are my sighs
When life takes its toll
On the me and the you
I remember my feelings
When we started a new
So take heart my darling
I will always be there
In a look in a feeling, in time
For I care.

June Woodward Martin

Untitled

Notes

I came to poetry fairly late in life, having hated it at school. Karen was a dear friend who, sadly, died at the age of 35. she is still greatly missed.

Karen, dear Karen
How long since you left me?
Days? Months? Years?
The fifth of May
I'm told.
It feels like
The fifth of never.
Were you really here?
Did you walk?
Did you speak to me?
Speak to me now
Dear Karen,
For I miss you so.

Frank Coldwell

Every Time

Every time you touch me,
my heart cries out for more.
Every time you kiss me,
it makes me want you more.
Every time we're parted
It feels like an eternity.
Every time we're reunited,
I am in paradise.
Every time that we make love
I feel waterfalls inside me.
Every time you look at me
I know it's yours I'll always be.

Patricia Heard

Ironically, for a book about love and relationships, this poem is about when you see something you want real bad and someone gets there before you. Although I have used the images of a girl, myself and another man and brought in this love element. But this can apply to being the geek in class who has a crush on this girl, who is then asked out by the most popular guy in the whole school, in front of you. The other point is that this poem wasn't written about anyone, although this person I know refuses to believe it.

This is another poem from my poems page of my web page

http://members.tripod.com/-Beat/poems.htm

and in my eyes the best one I have ever written, although I am sure some of you will slate it. I write poetry just for the enjoyment, sure there are 68 poems on my web page, *Emptiness* was also published, in *Word of Mouth* and is proving to be an excellent doorstop, only kidding. I enjoy reading it from time to time as I find that you out there have some excellent ways of conveying your feelings through poetry, and I think some of them are really top notch.

It's nice to finally see this poem published as I wanted it published the first time but it didn't quite fit the book's criteria. And I hope you get the same pleasure reading it that I do.

I am now 22, still reading Computer Studies at the University of Glamorgan, and still with the same interests.

As I Sit Beside the Window . . .

As I sit beside the window,
And look into the world,
My eyes float past the trees,
And focus on a girl.

Standing there alone,
With her never-ending hair,
She looks just like an angel,
Floating in the air.

I thought to go and talk,
To her, to ask her her name,
But I thought of the reply,
That I get again and again.

The grace in the movement,
As she walked round the road,
Made my heart collapse,
Underneath the great load.

As she turned round,
The sunlight bounced off her face,
I took a quick glance,
And my blood began to race.

I knew I was in love,
But it stopped very soon,
A man came round the corner,
And her eyes twinkled like the moon.

She kissed him and hugged him,
He welcomed the embrace,
It looked rather passionate,
And sorrow crossed my face.

As they walked down the road,
Walking hand in hand,
I moved away from the window,
And my heart turned into sand.

M Britt

I Knew

I think I knew quite early on,
You started to dress more carefully,
     and there was a spring in your step.
It wasn't anything specially that you said,
        . . . but I knew.

I found you looking at yourself in the mirror
       and exercising your face.
You fingered your parting and examined your hair
      and you seemed far away.

Then, through the kitchen window, I saw you
Laugh in the greenhouse, shake your head,
      ponder and smile,
As if musing over a repeated joke.
Something you had shared
      . . . but not with me.

You weren't unkind,
You didn't pick a quarrel, sulk or bicker.
But you weren't *there* anymore
      . . . and I *knew*.

Shirley Dyer

74

Notes

I began writing poetry in my
twenties and last year cele-
brated my eightieth birthday.
The early poems were mainly
light, humorous verse or
verses to celebrate anniver-
saries. Since my retirement,
however, my output has in-
creased and I have attempted
other verse forms. Two years
ago, I joined the poetry group
of our local U3A (University
of the Third Age) which gave
added impetus to my writing.

I try to adapt my style to the
subject of the poem. *What is
Love?* is a rare attempt at
blank verse.

As to my career, after leaving
University I worked for a
time as a research chemist,
but then switched to editing
and translating scientific ar-
ticles and books. For eighteen
years, I worked as a technical
editor for the World Health
Organisation in Geneva.

What is Love?

You ask me 'What is love?' and I reply
No single answer will, methinks, suffice,
For love takes many forms. Is it not strange
To grace by that same name, that selfsame name,
The bond that binds a mother to her child
And the tumultuous passion that torments
The callow youth bewitched by maiden's smiles
And drunk on the ambrosia of her lips?

A man's love for his brother we applaud,
For what could be a nobler sentiment?
Yet we deplore the love male friends profess,
Believing this transgresses Nature's law.
The Bible teaches man to love his neighbour,
Though coveting a neighbour's wife's a sin:
Great is the love that seeks not to possess,
While lust as love may never masquerade.

To like is not to love nor love to like,
For love's not blind to faults but faults forgives;
Many's the maid who loves a handsome rogue,
A knave whose erring ways she seeks to mend,
But when she fails she loves him yet the more;
And many's the man whose unrequited love
Feeds on the favours of some femme fatale,
Though of her wanton wiles he's well aware.

We may love music, poetry or art,
We may love Nature and the open road,
We love to dream and search for deeper meanings
In Life, in Love and in God's Master Plan.
One thing is sure: God's Plan on love depends,
For God, *is* Love and through love shapes our lives,
Do not then Love by baser names demean,
Nor in its stead promote the selfish gene!

Aubrey Woolman

Notes

Born in 1969 I now live in Devon with my son, Francis following my divorce.

My hobbies and interests vary from donkeys and children to needlecraft and reading.

I have scribbled for most of my life, but only within the last fifteen years have my scribbles shaped themselves into poetry.

so much can inspire me, sun on leaves, a raging sea, a long-forgotten memory, anything really.

I would like to dedicate 'Marriage - What is it?' to Diana, Princess of Wales for she was always an inspiration to me.

Marriage ~ What is it?

What is marriage if not
A self-restricting state
Between two people only
From the wedding date?
What if they find themselves
Not yet in love along the line;
Or maybe in love with another,
What can they do but pine?
Is marriage really necessary,
Or is it just outdated?
The worry over what to wear -
Or will the bride be late;
And if the bride on time is;
What next - four kids?
With the groom down at the pub
And the lovematch on skids,
Is marriage not just
A state of mind for persons two
When they think and feel alike,
In whatever they may do?
Is a piece of paper
Really quite essential,
When, after all, the novelty
Of marriage may just pall.

J E Alban

Funny How

Notes

My name is Stephen Williams. I'm 43 years of age, I have a wife Carole and a baby daughter named Anna. since the last time I wrote my Poet's Notes in *Word of Mouth* I have had three more poems published (other than this one) the first in an International Journal regarding Child Migration, the second in a book of poems called *20th Century Verse* and the third in a general anthology, *Just another Day*. I hope you enjoy my poem, if you can get your tongue round it!

It's funny how you grow together
Your lives become intertwined together
You're here together there together
Rarely wined and dined together
You're far too intertwined together
To gather that together can be rather wide apart

Maybe you walk together
But do you really, really, talk together
Not about the weather together
But your deep down thoughts together
Are you beginning to gather
That together is rather wide apart

Yes I know you sleep together
But do you go to bed together
Has the haven of your love together
pulled you more apart than together
all the things that brought you together
As you can gather can force you wide apart

Stephen Williams

Notes

All my poems are dedicated
to my late wife Jean (Jenny),
and to the good people of
Porthleven, Near Helston,
Cornwall, who have made me
so welcome in this wonderful
little fishing port. God Bless
them all.

Lost Love

She gave to me a flower
a rose of deepest red
she stayed with me an hour
then with my heart she fled
I've searched the whole world over
and scoured each leafy lane
my heart it bleedeth over
till we shall meet again

If you should see a vision' sir
a true wonder to behold
please tell her that I love her
until my heart grow cold
and if she knows the tragedy
she left within my heart
then perhaps she will return to me
and never more we'll part

I still cherish the flower
though faded it may be
and I am counting every hour
till she returns to me
but if she has found another
there is nought that I can do
except to say, I love her
and will, my whole life through.

D Baker

I Loved You

As the nights grew longer I looked towards the sky
There were so many stars shining equally bright
After a while one began to glow
I stared so hard and wanted to know
How I could reach that beautiful star
I was anxious and scared of going so far
If only it would fall down to me
I would catch it and hold it close to me
So days went by and there I was
As eager as ever and never cross
I had waited too long for it began to show
That my star ceased to glow.

Jamil Alam

Fantasy

Notes

Have you ever walked into a
crowded room holding just
one person? A velvet hush
surrounds you as the most
beautiful girl you've ever
seen glides into a slow turn.
You hold her in your eyes as
her head turns and for a split
second, you think she notices
you.

This is what I wrote when it
happened to me and I still
wish it were a dream so I
could pretend she saw me.
Yet, isn't love what dreams
are made of?

She stands tall and beautiful.
She glides graceful and shines bright.
She looks round, her eyes gleam,
And she looks straight past me
And smiles.

I wished so much that she
Could see and look at me -
Now I think that she
Never did see
How I feel about her.

And now, perhaps, I see
That maybe I made myself believe
That the glint in her
Eyes was for me.

So now again in my
Heart and in my mind
I am alone and bereft
Of hope for love

For the only girl
I've known who has been able
To see how I feel
Inside without words,
Is gone.

But then, perhaps,
This too, I convinced
Myself of and so,
Now I see, perhaps
All my hopes and
Dreams are and ever
Will be . . .
Fantasy.

Wait!
Is she?

Richard Cassidy

Notes

An actor by profession, I wrote *Content Avenue* while doing a Rep season in Scotland, On the avenue was the theatre, and it felt appropriate to name the poem after it as it tied itself into my thoughts nicely at the time.

My wife is expecting our first child in January 1998 and we are both looking forward to the occasion.

Content Avenue

If you think of me while I am away, don't be sad;
Just play back the memories of all the good times we have had.

Love is a myriad word and I often see it in your eyes, my love,
Forever holding you, entwined around your body, soft white as a dove.

When we come together again and emptiness is filled with pleasure,
Take your time to kiss my mouth and let feelings take you at our leisure.

You may remember me at every moment, every heartbeat of your life;
So I go on thinking of you, wanting you, my miracle of a wife.

Jeffrey Bird

Untitled

Notes

Written in the autumn of my life with a catalogue of romantic disasters behind me and a firm conviction that love was not destined for me.

This poem is dedicated to the very special person who was my unexpected and ever-treasured destiny. It comes from my soul for my soul-mate.

The Moon spins out my spirit
In an arc that stretches out to spatial shores
And somewhere up there
In the black brilliance of the skies
My soul meets up with yours -
Fuses, forges, and thus fixed
Becomes one whole again - and flies
Soaring, untrammelled, through the portals of the galaxy
In that unforgettable orbit of ecstasy
Which once we two, mere mortals,
Did chance to share;
While I, an empty shell, weightless as air
Remain transfixed -
Rooted to the earth by dreaming eyes,
Waiting for that tidal-wave of feeling
To lap me as your thoughts of love come flooding
Helter-skelter
Through each vein
To take away - for one brief souls' encounter -
The bitter ache of pain.

Diane Lyle

Fate

Ours was a brief encounter
A once in a lifetime chance
Your presence quite overwhelmed me
And wrapped me up in a trance.

We talked, we were silent - what matter,
No words could describe what we felt,
But we couldn't indulge our affections,
Because of the cards we were dealt.

You returned to your old life much wiser,
I had to start over again,
But we both knew we'd always be haunted
By the thought of just 'what might have been'

What mad twist of fate kept us parted
Insistent we play out dull roles,
And squander the riches and passions
Of two so alike kindred souls.

Sadie Smyth

Farewell

Notes

I started writing at primary
school, where I thoroughly
enjoyed creating characters
and story lines. It was not
until 1994, when I was 14,
that I wrote my first piece of
poetry. During the following
years, as a GCSE student, I
wrote many more poems on
various topics. I am currently
studying poetry as part of my
English Literature A Level
course.

Now I am 17, many of my
poems are inspired my close
network of friends, music,
and current world issues.
This is the seventh poem I
have had published, one was
also included on a cassette
recording.

Two silhouettes
Meeting in the dark,
Saying a passionate goodbye,
And letting go of their hearts.
In their eyes you can see memories gone by,
And dreams that were never meant to be,
Those that will remain for always un petit rêve
Slip out of their hands like rocks to the sea
Nothing left to say,
except that word of goodbye
Their last word, their last breath
To a love that's died.
So not a word they say,
They just kiss gently
Then walk away, as their passion has gone,
And a single wave disappears into the sea.

Emma Louise Nyman

The Ice Man

Cold and distant standing like a lifeless statue
ice white and with blue eyes staring into oblivia
what is it he is thinking about I wish I could know
I can never get close - I stand alone in the sunlight
feeling the warmth on my skin caressing my hands

While he stands in cold where the light fades
and where it is too cold to try and reach to
Ignoring my sudden movement - I do not exist
in his eyes I am past tense of something trivial
something slightly humorous but oh not to love

Coldness of his voice and eyes prick my eyes
and counteract against the burning flames of mine
He stands in an ice cold palace I can never get to
Waiting for her to give him a hint of a glimpse
But she hurries on and does not see what I see

His ice cold heart ready to melt just for her
the pale white face would break into a smile
if she looked at him but it's all in such vain
while I gaze on stupidly waiting for his smile
This precious smile but to me it never comes

So I continue to wait in such forlorn hope
he might feel cold and come to me to warm
But for the moment the ice man feels no cold
and continues his dying vigil to gain her love
while I wait in the shadows alone and - too warm

Amber Gardner

Nobody's Fool

Now you've filled my heart with hate
I am hard and hollow,
You've put too much on my plate
And it's hard to swallow,
Now you're turning away from me
Don't think I'll follow.
The act is over now
So close the curtain,
I don't think that this is so,
I know for certain
That you are simply not worth
All of this hurting.
For now the tears have left my eyes
I can see you clearly,
I could now make you think twice,
But you won't hear me.
If you take my advice
You won't dare come near me.
For all that we have become
Is a burnt out candle,
And although you've gone cold,
You're too hot to handle.
You've left my heart in pieces,
. . . Vandal!

Jay Hollis

Notes

I was born in Cleethorpes, currently residing in Cheshire, missing the sea!

I feel privileged to have another poem in print.

Married for 28 years to David, we have faced the 'high seas', and so far survived.

Proudly, I state that my daughter Elvina (my critic) was successful in achieving her 'A' levels - English Literature being one of them.

Since 1980 I have nursed and cared for my lovely mother, Lilian Stockwood.

I am presently in my third year, developing some skills as a counsellor.

Love, What is it?

Is this love I ask myself?
How do you tell?
Longer than lust,
I know this well.

So my heart's pounding,
when our eyes meet,
I've lost my logic,
I cannot speak.

We seem in tune,
is he my soul mate?
Was it love at first sight?
As he entered the room.

With time, will I ever know?
Will we dance the same dance,
is this called love?
Will it blossom and grow

Life is a puzzle,
why are we here?
To give love, to find love,
is lasting love rare?

Well, I suppose we'll never know,
but, one thing is clear,
better to have loved and lost,
than to have never loved - this
I hold dear!

Gill Barratt

You

You are the coat
That keeps out the storm;
You are the hearth
That always glows warm;
To the locked doorway
You are the key;
For the wide river
You are the sea;
In the grand ballroom
You are the dancer;
To the last question
You are the answer;
After cold Winter
You are the Spring;
Here on my finger
You are the ring;
Where there is music
You are the song;
You can make better
All that is wrong;
Rising at morning
You are the lark;
You are the sunlight
Piercing the dark;
After the nightmare
You are tomorrow;
You are a promise
Healing the sorrow;
You are the swan
On the wings of the wind;
You are forgiveness
When I have sinned;
You are my light
And my joy and my friend
As we travel a journey
That never will end.

Andrew Tweed

Notes

Nothing pleases me more than to be able to create a poem specifically for an individual. It is something that is unique to the individual, something they can keep forever.

Along with the artistry, created by my daughter Gill, we find we share a God given talent, and something we hope to explore.

Only the hardship I have suffered has brought enhancement to a gift, for in all I learned, there I found wisdom. As always my heartfelt thanks is given to God for giving me this wonderful gift.

To my daughter Gill, whom I love with all my heart, to my parents, my aunt and Uncle, to James and always in memory of my son Andrew, who has been with the Lord for almost twelve years, without these individuals, I would not be so rich.

To those who have given me the means to take my message to the world. I send my heartfelt thanks.

Touch Me

Touch me with a smile,
To brighten my day.
Bring love and laughter
Let them not, slip away.
In a world of unhappiness
And utmost despair.
Give me a smile.
Show me, you care.

Touch me with compassion
Let sympathy prove.
That in this love action
It may help me move.
For a heart that's been broken,
With others will blend.
Pouring on balm,
To help others, to mend.

Touch me with company
Let friendship increase.
May caring and sharing
And love, never cease.
Be now the bond
That helps others to love.
Touched by the heavenly,
Grace: from above.

Touch me with love,
Then I may know.
All of the fruitfulness
As you help me grow.
Lord in your mercy
May my heart be true.
Always, and only
Set, radiantly, on you.

Janet Parry

Notes

This is my sixty-first piece of work which has been accepted for publication.

My poems have appeared in various anthologies for Arrival Press, Anchor Books and Triumph House - all based in Peterborough. I have also reached the semi-final stage in eight national poetry competitions.

I have recently become a distinguished member of the International Poetry Society.

Nothing in Common

'We've nothing in common', you said,
Yet still I shared your bed.
Nothing in common to share,
No hobbies, interests to compare.
No, nothing but love for each other,
Nothing useful to keep us together.
We must have long periods apart.
But you're always in my heart
'We've nothing in common', you said,
But still I've shared your bed.

Susan Mullinger

Promises

You've left me sitting here,
All on my own again,
Your promises mean nothing,
they wash away in the rain,
I used to be free,
I used to be young,
Now I'm trapped,
Because I can't breathe without my lung,
You take what you can,
You leave when you choose,
You take me to heaven,
Then you laugh as I lose,
You think I can't live,
Without you to hold my hand,
But your words lie on the beach,
The tide washed them away in the sand.
You tell me how much you care,
Say I'm so beautiful,
And when I say I love you,
You smile as you lie.
I'm so mad at you,
Because the phone doesn't ring,
You said you'd call,
You said I meant something,
But your promises glide into the distance,
Your face once my salvation,
I can't stand to think about,
Because it will be just another con,
So goodnight sweetheart,
As you drift away in your lies
I'll turn my eyes away,
As I watch the grey skies.

G E Parry

First Kiss

The arranging for a date,
Then the praying he better not be late.
I had fancied him for so long,
Please God don't let anything go wrong.

Of course there was cross wires somewhere,
I wonder would he like my hair.
It's took me three hours to get dressed,
I only want him to see me at my very best.

No one told me I could feel so good,
Those butterflies in my stomach lifted my mood.
Oh no my nail broke, I hope he doesn't see,
What if he wants me to sit on his knee.

We were so excited when we met,
I broke out in an all-over sweat.
The first kiss was so sweet,
If lifted me right off my feet.

The joy and the happiness we both shared,
It's like nothing else to compare.
When I feel low I think of this,
Such a joy I am glad I did not miss,
That wonderful exciting first kiss.

April Uprichard

Without You

An hour without you
Is an hour without light,
The mind loses its cue
And colour turns black and white.

Don't be away for long:
The measuring of time
Kills the joy in my song;
Without you I'm a mime!

When you are not there
The void stares at me,
The rooms are all bare
And I am all at sea.

Without you, night is long
And day is not a cure,
When all seems to go wrong
How much can I endure?

A year without you
Is a year without life
Or beauty to woo -
Just nothing but strife!

What is life
Without you
My dear!

F van Haelewyck

Something to Regret

You call out to me in my dreams
And I await you longingly
I see you coming through the night
I want something that we'll both regret
Come the morning light
But as for now just hold me tight

You'll soon discover your love gone sour
For me when you realise what happened
But until then drink up my friend
And give yourself something to regret . . .
Come the morning light
Don't hold back
Don't try to fight
Give me something to hate myself for.

Hazel Aldridge

Notes

I am 31 years old and have one brother. We are a close family and my parents are very supportive. My occupation is that of a nurse and I have worked for the past 14 years in the NHS. I have lived in Norfolk for six years and will soon be moving to North Lincolnshire in the new year.

This is my second poem to be published and I am in the process of researching for a novel (fantasy).

I started writing poetry at school and have a great fondness for Scotland very inspirational. I have a family history of Scottish descent.

Knowing You are There

No longer do I sit and stare
At the pages white and bare
It all now flows so easily
Knowing you are there
The words I've searched so long to find
Now wander freely through my mind
They tumble down so easily
Knowing you are there
I know that you will be there
To kiss away each tear I cry
To help me and support me
In each new venture that I try
It's written in the runes and stars
Together we will both go far
I know that you'll be there for me
In everything I touch and see
So watch out world and be prepared
To see the love that we now share
It fits together perfectly
Knowing you'll be there

D M Roads

Love

Love not too lightly lest the passing years
Reveal your love as but a fickle thing
Of little worth, so full of doubts and fears
'Twill fail against the trials that life will bring.

If love you will then set foundations well,
With constancy and honour, strongly built;
What storms each dawn may bring no one can tell:
By standing firm such love can never wilt.

Deflect not from the true and steadfast way,
When evil tempts, your pledge of love recall,
To succour with compassion day by day,
To share the pain and grief should ills befall.

Two lives are one when love's twixt man and wife,
So he who has not loved lives half a life.

Reginald E Miles

Decisions

Through my tears I see you wonder,
I sense your silent pain,
Uncertain what to do now,
Unclear of who will gain.
I scream to seek some comfort,
I fight to free my heart,
Logic will lose and leave me,
Love plays the stronger part.
I close my eyes to calm me,
But I only see her face.
Haunted by her memory.
I need to find some space.
I run but cannot hide now,
Her voice still in my head,
I need to find myself now,
My will is almost dead.
My love for you will help me,
Her voice will turn to yours.
I'm strong enough to beat that
I've fought in crueller wars.
My destiny imprisoned,
You're the holder of the key,
Decide which path to follow,
Your history or me.
The pain will not escape us,
The stakes may seem too high,
Fear the future, but face forwards,
It can happen if you try.
Rise up and seize your freedom,
Reclaim the hurt and tears.
Seek solace in being my comfort,
Only you can kill your fears.

Michelle Bradley

Something Missing

Notes

Andy Botterill is a 32 year old trained journalist, presently working in arts administration. He started writing poetry at about 18 and his poems and stories have appeared widely in the small press magazines in this country and abroad. His other interests include sport, film and music.

He was happy once,
And then she left him.
He didn't know when
He was onto a good thing.
That was his problem.

They had a house.
He bought her a kitten,
Showered her with gifts, love,
And then took them back again.

They used to go to town
On a Saturday evening.
They drank until they could hold no more,
And it was fun.

Sometimes they would stay in.
They would buy fish and chips
And eat them
In front of the television.

Later they would make love
With the light on,
And they would talk
Till night became morning.

He knew how to hold her attention.
That is until she found another man.
Suddenly she stopped giving.
She stopped being so open.

She said she needed something new
To open up her horizon.
She said he was no longer the person
He'd once been.
It was hard to take in.

Now he is alone.
He thinks of her from time to time,
Remembers the days they spent together,
But all in all,
He's got used to her not being there.

He's met other women,
But somehow they weren't the same.
He tries to make it work,
But something's always missing.

Andrew Botterill

Notes

I have been writing poetry for about 14 years and have been fortunate to have had quite a few published. One ambition in life is to have a complete book of my own works published.

Amateur photography, gardening, and also writing and producing personalised cards for all occasions are among my numerous hobbies and interests.

This year I have been blessed with my first grandchild, a wonderful little girl named Chloe.

My inspiration comes from the beauty around me, and it is my way of expressing my innermost thoughts and feelings.

Unspoken Words

What's in my heart, in my mind, I find so hard to say,
As I awake - before I sleep - I search to find a way.
To express my love, my feelings, they will never fade,
Life for me, its meaning - only you alone have made.
The joy, the warmth I feel, whenever you are near,
You are my inspiration, and forever - very dear.
You give me strength and courage, to face what lies ahead,
We do not have to speak, for our unspoken words are said.
You say you do so little, loving me - you do so much,
A smile, that special look - I love your gentle touch.
One day those unspoken words, will be spoken and evolve,
Always my thoughts - my dreams - around you will revolve.

Irene J Mooney

The Call

Watching, waiting.
Listening for that moment.
All is quiet. All is still.
On goes the telly.
Not really watching.
The pictures go right through me.
Is that -
No. Just part of the storyline.
There it goes -
Rush, rush;
Deep breath; telly off,
'Ring' 'Ring'
Is it her?
'Hello!'
Yes.

R J Poynter

Notes

I dedicate this poem to the Lady of the museum, Angela M Rafferty FMPM.

Angela FMPM

You are on my mind and in my dreams,
Please please lady, just stop awhile, and
Give time, to cast me a smile,

My tortured and agile mind cannot erase recent
Pleasant memories, at your features and your face
I gaze in delight, my little legs prevent me giving chase,

I guess there's a decade of years between us by far,
Age - a myth! Frustrated feelings, please give me time,
You move around so quickly 'lanky legs!' It turns me a little sickly,

No time to spare, to ascertain, 'Am I your special friend?'
Who knows, who really cares, apart from me, so
Make me happy, to me be caring, do not drive me around the bend,

Because my dear, words can never say it all,
Especially if one's heart is smitten
And it does not matter what is written, as
Much has past and beyond recall.

Duncan Robson

Beasts in Love

The silhouette of two rising souls,
Against a skyline so deep and red,
The golden waves crash at their feet,
As their giant hooves rear to a head.

No sound can be heard except their cries,
As ecstasy they have found,
Galloping through the broken waves,
To a destiny by which they are both bound.

The silent sound of thudding hooves,
Pounding out at the sand,
As they race toward their final goal,
And seal each soul by their only band.

The way of making two souls into one
The only way the beast of the earth know,
As, unlike, us, we have our love,
To keep watch as our hearts grow.

And so the simple way seems to bind,
Two horses at the water's edge,
And until they both meet the end,
At least *they* will keep their pledge.

Melanie Lane

Notes

For just over two years poetry
has been a source of surprise
and delight. I have recently
had my first small collection
of Christian verse published.

It is a familiar experience
that in times of emotional
stress or joy it is therapeutic
to write down one's feelings.
This poem is such an example
and one of many I have
written on the same theme.
When I lost someone very
dear to me I worked through
many stages of grief. Even
after six years the memories
are still strong and will re-
main so.

Memories of You

After six long years I still see your face
Smiling at me and I can't help but long
For the sweet music of your voice again,
Speaking the worlds of our beautiful song.

I remember some of the things you loved:
Blackcurrants, pink blossomed horse chestnut trees;
Hiawatha, Mozart and Yorkie bars,
And autumn's glory never failed to please.

There were places we loved to call our own;
When I hear 'our song' you will never know
How my heart ebbs and flows much like the sea
And a rising tide of memories flow.

Who could tell the pain would last for so long?
The cold fingers of grief gripped me so tight
Extinguishing all the light of our love,
And my life was one continuous night.

You must let him go, friends lovingly urged.
You're sad, of course, you have a need to mourn,
But don't sink too low so your spirit dies,
Welcome a new life that's waiting to dawn.

So now when my heart overflows with tears,
They gently wash precious moments we knew;
I gather them fondly, each one caressed
Like the flowers kissed by the morning dew.

I lift a corner of my heart to find
A host of sweet memories lingering there,
Your sweet laughter echoes and softly falls
Like shafts of sunbeams floating in the air.

Mary Care

No Where . . .

The intention was there,
It really was.
It was there,
But I wasn't.

I meant to go
But I didn't get there.
I'm not sure why, it
just happened that way.

No excuses, no lies.
The way it is,
the way it died.

And here we are.
The intention's still there
But, wherever it is,
I am not.

I know I should go
And now the distance is there.
It's growing and growing.
It's too far away
With time and space the distance
is too great.
With life itself it's just
too late.

Katie Marks

Earth's Lament

The wind pierced the blackened sky,
And sang thru' the window's frame,
She was sad and so cried out,
Her tears the pouring rain,

Yet in the comfort of her arms,
I thought that I could sense,
Nature screaming out for help,
As her last line of defence,
Began to show that time was near,
For us to understand,
That if we turned away our ears,
She'd take back all her land.

The subtle execution, not plague or
Wars of blood,
But silent raindrops filling,
The towns with waves of flood,

River, streams were swallowed whole,
And lakes turned into seas,
Waiting for the ice maiden,
Who brings the winter freeze.
But days and weeks soon they passed,
And still she'd not appeared,
And lives were swept away like dust,
And swathes of trees were cleared.

Making way for us to act,
And mend what she had done,
The soothing breeze of an April day,
Or summer's warming sun,
Seemed like distant memories,
But time will heal the scars,
So why can't we take care of her,
And love what's truly ours.

P N Hope

Notes

Married for forty - five years(!) at the age of 64, having been mother to five children, I am now grandmother to twelve, which of course, is lovely. We live in a tiny village up in the hills outside Dover. In 1996 we won, by combined community efforts, the title of Best Kept Village in Kent.

For nearly twenty six years I was school dinner lady at the local (next village!) Shepherdswell School. I originally trained as a librarian, a wonderful job as I love books.

As a small child, I wrote poetry of a sort, and during the past five years I have, at long last, been published by Arrival Press at Peterborough. I use many different styles, rhyming, blank, free; but I always try for 'scanning'.

Prizes? Nil! However, I write for our church magazine and also the community magazine in the next village, Elvington. The Dover Express also accepts my work, either community news or the St John's Ambulance notes.

Hobbies include embroidery (very soothing after a busy day), reading of course and all my lovely grandchildren.

Inspiration can come from absolutely anything, from unnerving waits at the dentist, seaside picnics, boot fairs - all is grist for the mill.

Earlier this year, after nearly ten years research, I published the history of our village, the Coldred Chronicle, which was very well received, and has been selling really well.

Finally, let Longfellow have the last word:

Music is the universal language of mankind, poetry their universal pastime and delight

First Love

An August afternoon of careless splendour,
The joyaunce of that first delightful kiss!
An ecstasy of spirit beatific,
A hot-mouthed ravishment of long remembered bliss!

Love, by definition, is the tune,
Played by many a piper slain by Cupid's dart.
Old age and youth go hand in hand with rapture.
Who cares for winter, when ascendant summers in the heart!

Marjorie Chapman

Someone So Special

You are someone so special who I could never ever ignore,
And I can see my entire future in your lovely face,
You always make me feel ever so safe and so secure,
And with you darling, my life is firmly set into place.

You are my summer, my winter, my autumn and spring.
You are my whole world, and I would give you everything.
I am complete when you are in my arms, so lovingly,
And your love will stay with me for all of eternity.

Stephen Clark

To My Husband. My Valentine

Skilled writers and great poets have written verse and prose
Comparing love with music, or like a deep red rose.
And we know love is precious, and we know that its worth
Can't be compared with anything that's to be found on earth.

For you have known great sadness, upon life's waves been tossed,
And felt the pain of suffering with loved ones you have lost.
Now days are full of sweetness, you're free from all alarms,
For you have found a shelter within my loving arms.

I had been very lonely, and longed to share a home.
And felt just like a mariner on stormy seas - alone.
But when a storm is over, and the sun shines from above
So I have come to rest dear, in the harbour of your love.

The majesty of mountains, and the mystery of the sea,
The cool shade in a summer wood - that's what you are to me,
For you are all the strength I need, when I am tired and weak,
You stand so strong and resolute, the safety that I seek.

Like the sunshine of each day that dawns, our gold along life's path
The sweet peace of contentment, that we find beside our hearth.
These then are our riches, a happy carefree home
Where seeds of laughter, trust and love forever have been sown.

And so you have this heart of mine,
My husband dear, my Valentine.

Angela Douse

Our Path of Love

This poem is to be dedicated to all those who have found love, a love so real that it has been able to survive not only the good times but also the bad and rough.

Our Path of Love looks deep into the theme of true love. One may ask themselves 'Is there such a thing as true love?' However, love is true, as this poem aims to show, when two people, special to one another have been able to form a special kind of love through continuously supporting each other regardless, having these times or memories strengthen their desire to secure the other one's needs when the going gets tough. Such inseparable lives characterise the title of the poem *Our Path of Love*.

We have travelled
This far on
Our path of love
With the
Footsteps of
Our memories
Behind us.
They will
Continue to follow,
Become our history,
Become
The most visible mark
Of our mutual love.

Hand in hand
We walk,
Our affection
Our hopes
Secured
By this touch.
My eyes in yours
Yours in mine
Our hearts
Speak
Through our
Endless stare.

Lost
We always become
When our
Feelings take over,
Lift us high,
Awaken our inner lives.

Our path of love
Is the root of us,
The soul of
Our memories -
Our past,
Present
And future
Together
As one.

Natalie Robinson

Love's Seasons

Notes

This is my second published poem. I'm delighted to see this in print as it was written for the love of my life - my husband, Harvey, to whom I have been married for 28 wonderful years.

We are lovers, confidantes and great friends, who share every joy and sorrow, but most of all an immense sense of fun and laughter.

If our spring, summer and autumn years are any yardstick, God willing our winter will be a 'cracker'!

Whispered words in moments tender
Looks exchanging secret thoughts
Soft caresses, breathless pledges,
Youth and hope dispelling doubt.
As new life bursts forth in season,
Flowering seed and tree in bud,
So our hearts began their journey
Through the springtime of our love.

Plans and dreams, we shaped the future,
No hill too high for us to climb,
Bells proclaiming, rings exchanging,
Separate lives are now entwined.
As the sunlight burns eternal
In the cloudless heavens above
So our hearts were fired with passion
In the summer of our love.

Lives are full, but days grow shorter,
Leaves upon the trees turn gold.
Grain is garnered for the winter,
Flowers fade and nests grow cold.
As hearth fires glow with burnished embers
Winds stir smoky skies above
So our hearts are warmed with memories
In the autumn of our love.

Seasons change, time waits for no man,
Snowy thatch and withered boughs,
Was it only yesterday
We stood and made forever vows.
As springtime jewels sleep 'neath the cold earth
Awakening with the warmth above
So our hearts await the calling
To the winter of our love.

Kath Wiles

Opposites

Smiling face,
Menacing frown,
Serious pose,
Act the clown,
Working hard,
Time for play,
Silent mind,
Lots to say,
Body weary,
Full of life,
Blunt as stone,
Sharp as a knife,
Wanting to fight,
Need for peace,
Extremely tense,
A great release,
Black as night,
White as snow,
Heading nowhere,
Go with the flow,
Chant with the moon,
Sing in the sun,
Total regret,
Full of fun,
Calm on a pond,
Rough as the sea,
Yin and Yang for life to be,
Born in the wild,
Pleasantly tame,
We're total opposites and exactly
The same.

Michelle Jeffrey

Summer Love

Back to back in the hedgerow
June sun in the sky
Sheep in the meadow, songbirds on high
Tall barley swaying in the cool breeze
Like waves of the ocean, tall and green

The feeling of passion as fingers entwine
knowing that never would he be mine
Just savour the moment, be it short or long
something so sweet cannot be wrong

Oh exquisite pain, is this love?
My heart a flutter like wings of a dove
I'll never forget my day in the sun
with him beside me making my blood run

I know this can't last, I know it will end
but it will not be over we will still be friends
Never to walk in the country again
Just to close my eyes tight, and pretend

Jean Dunn

Your Hands

Restless Hands
fidgeting
moving
stroking
not finding
peace
restless hands
touching a ring
can't
feel at ease
restless hands
soft and
weary
hands to trust
hands so gentle
how I loved
those
restless hands

L R Mitchell

Love That Makes You Glow

Love makes you glow in the dark.
You shine like a candle
That will not burn out.
You touch many people
Whose lives, are so full of doubt.
Giving them hope
To still carry life out.

Remember, remember.
It's a gift from above.
Not given lightly
But to those that love.
Love keeps you striving
All along the way.
Hope never ending
Whatever the day.
Through rain and heavy clouds
You keep going on.
Hoping and praying
That one day, you will find.
That treasure of treasures,
You thought you had left behind.

Myrna M Bailey

Love

Notes

This little poem was written in the Spring of 1973 following the loss of my beloved dad. The previous Autumn my husband had planted an old horse trough with poly-anthus outside our kitchen window.; they seemed to pass a little message of hope to me every time they revived from a storm -when the sun shone through. They warmed my heart which had been cold all that Winter.

I thought that love was like a tender flower.
That must be nurtured in a sheltered bower.
But it must be fed by warmth and rain
From smiles of joy and tears of pain
If it's to grow and reach its finest hour.

I watched the flowers that bloomed in early springtime
They blossomed on a warm and sunny day,
Then winter storms came back again -
They were lashed with wind and snow and rain,
(They must have felt such hurt and pain)
I thought they'd never rise to live again
But after every fall of snow they seemed to have an added glow,
And strength to lift their heads and smile again.
I thought dear God! That's true
That's just what life is all about
We take the bitter blows that come with love
We feel the pain and sorrow
But we smile to face tomorrow
With strength that seems to flow from up above.

Hilary Richardson

Notes

I am a 23 year old student at the University of Westminster studying English and Inter-disciplinary studies. I would like to publish an anthology quite soon. As well as writing I also paint and I am very in-terested in Art history.

This poem is not about ro-mantic love but hope and trust which should be treas-ured.

I dedicate this poem in loving memory of the Angel that was my sister Colette.

Just a Second

Give me your direction and maybe we'll meet,
another time a different direction same street
You keep to the left I veer to the right
should you lose your footing and tumble with might
we bless ourselves and keep to the light.

With the characteristics of either yet the character of none
we continue on our journey from whence it begun

It was about the next turning that I stumbled and cut my heart
broken in six places torn apart
We found a quiet spot that I might rest,
I remember you tried to distract me and performed with great jest
But still my heart it could not mend
and remained in tatters torn and bent.

So I wrapped my heart up in your hand
and secured it with a golden band
Sending you on your way
to return to me the following day.
I lay my head down to rest
secure in the knowledge that you would do your best
And in my sleep I dreamt that we were drunk and that you fell
and we were satisfied but could not tell
Cause I always thought that I was empty
stood next to you, a heart so full of plenty

I longed to know that feeling that curious voluptuous feeling,
but still I remain the sea-bed whose ocean has retreated,
the moon stood too close to the sun uncomfortably over-heated

But in the morning when I awoke
I sheltered in your shadow and was immersed in hope
Your liquid eyes looked down into me
as you handed me a box with a golden key
And in that box I found my heart
no longer in six places torn apart.

Veronique Astwood

Notes

Freda Ringrose was born 19th September, 1920 and was a former War Widow. She has five sons.

She studied professional singing from the age of 16 until she retired. She has also done Auxiliary Nursing and worked in one of the Big Four Banks for 12 years.

On retiring, she was widowed for the second time whilst living in Surrey. She decided to uproot herself at the age of 68 and moved to Lincolnshire, where she started to discover that she had a flair for writing as a poet (she had always liked writing).

Her poems are mostly emotional; helped in some way by her singing career (as she tends to go into a coma when writing and acts out the part, then cannot remember one of the poems she has written: about 200 at the time of writing).

She has published her own book and raised a sum of money for a Scanner Appeal at the Pilgrim Hospital in Boston, Lincs.

Her first soldier husband is mostly the inspiration behind a lot of her writing and she has been told that people like her poems as they can understand them; they are in plain English!

She wrote a poem for the Dunblane disaster, which was published in the world-wide book by the Sun newspaper recently. Practically every poem she submits is accepted. Photography is another hobby.

Bewildered!

I think of you often and wonder why?
You were always so sad, and so easy did cry.
Teardrops that fell from your eyes as rain,
Saddened my heart -
Filled me with pain.

The urge to comfort grew stronger each day . . .
What could I do?
What could I say?

Our paths had crossed for a very short while,
Your presence enough to my face brought a smile.
Yet love was never to enter my mind -
My aim was never to be unkind.
Was I wrong to defy and ignore your need?
The need that from your eyes did plead!
Perchance, I happened not to be wise -
I broke a heart - a heart that did bleed
In its quest for love,
Yet help came not to my mind from above.
Tell me! Oh, tell me!
Why did I not see?
What could happen to me when I rejected your love!
I caused you much pain, but oh, that my chance
Could live over again.

Freda Ringrose

Notes

Poetry and high ideals mingle
inextricably, which is as it
should be. There are few of
us who do not have a vision
of an ideal partner and this
poem is such a vision.

*It is dedicated to a beautiful
woman who, to me, will al-
ways be* 'She'.

She

It was as though I slept but did not rest
Or laboured, unblessed,
Haunted by a face that was not there,
Blue eyes, fair hair.

The image faded yet returned again
With sweetness and pain,
A thousand thousand faces, how they blur!
But none like Her.

The sky grew darker with the passing years
Heavy with fears
That She was on some path which I had missed
Or did not exist.

Faith and hope, I thought that faith fell first
In hunger and thirst,
But hope had trod the path where faith had gone
And led me on.

Then came the light, a million candles power
At that dark hour
And it was She, the dawn to end the night
Who held the light.

Jack Crossman

Teen Love

Do you remember your first true love,
when you were just sixteen.
A love that never leaves you,
kept locked in your memory like a dream.

Walking hand in hand by the river,
stopping to hug and kiss.
Looking into each other's eyes,
as if no one else exists.

Finding somewhere quiet to be alone,
in a cornfield, or a wood.
Just to talk about yourselves,
about being together for good.

He gives her a token of his love,
she says she'll wear it forever.
He promises her undying love,
and never ever leave her.

Then his mates said come out tonight,
we are going to a club.
You are much too young to settle down,
leave her and come to the pub.

Soon it was all over,
although he loved her true.
She found herself another,
and her love for him grew.

She married and had children,
and sometimes she remembers.
The times they were together,
in her autumn years of September.

Jeanette Bunn

I Don't Love You

'I don't love you'
so you said
lying there upon the bed
where moments sooner love was made
or was it simply 'getting laid'

'I don't love you'
love's a pain
such feelings you could not sustain
keep it clean so when it breaks
nothings hurts and nothing aches

'I don't love you'
it's going nowhere
we don't have a life to share
just moments as and when we can
each time proving you're a man

'I don't love you'
that's OK
I don't love you anyway
I'll take my chances, trust in luck
and when I walk, you'll feel the buck

Marion Kemsley

Notes

Alexander Buchan was born in Bedford in 1958. He gained an Honours Degree in Philosophy at Sussex University, and worked, for several years, with people with learning difficulties. He left this to study Information Technology and then child care. He now writes poems and short stories.

He practices Buddhism of Nichiren Daishonin, chanting Nam-Myoho Renge-Kyo, and is influenced by T S Eliot, Sylvia Plath and Brian Patten. His poem, *Surfing the Storm Clouds*, is due to be published in the anthology, Jewels of the Imagination

Dedicated to lovers everywhere.

Falling Lovers

All attachment is transient, nothing is permanent
What you love can be snatched away
That's a fact and it's as plain as day

Death and the dollar, the shekel and the reaper
Dancing on a coffin with the dinara
I watched the pound go through the roof, only
to meet the undertaker when it came crashing down

Death and love intertwine
Falling in love can bring deep fear of death
Do you love me to death?
Or just until we part?
I'll just die if I don't see you tonight
Can you fall in love with death and is that the same as
being in love with loss?
Can you fall in love at death or is that just a case of lousy timing?

Let all tragic falling lovers
catch each other saving themselves from falling
by melting into each other's embrace
becoming one with the eternal ocean
feeling as waves breaking gently on the beach

Alexander Buchan

All there is,
Is the two of us,
And that's all we need.

Untitled

I am centred, focused,
words come from my pen that I have
not heard in my head.
She asks me about the phrasing of a
sentence for her paper.
Peppeting? Ethical review committees?
The topics are of little importance,
I know that look and it's infectious.
She's in a groove,
her words begin to flow,
calmly I answer and her head tilts back
down towards her work.
I can think, and the centre of the universe
is in this room between us.

Mark Friedman

Together Forever

You are a man every girl dreams for,
God had created a lot of men
But never created anyone like you before.
I always dream about you
I always want you to be mine,
If I wait my whole life for you
I know it won't be a waste of my time.
If I had to tell everyone how much I love you
I will not feel no shame,
I can cope with anything as long as
You don't cause me no pain.
You are going to be mine
As it seems only fair,
Nothing will come between us
And we will be together forever.

Sajeda Begum

Love's Orbits

Rocket like, love zooms from the soul
With such power it needs no hole
Yes now it's out to do some good
Surely as trees are made of wood

Because it's all around the world
Its time its secrets were unfurled
As it homes in on its target
Unique new forces now are set

A chain reaction makes a start
Right in the centre of the heart
All at a swiftly moving pace
Like runners in a relay race

Dispense some love for it is true
Other love will return to you
You've heard it makes the world go round
Yes, well its spring is fully wound

Now really it's not used enough
And that can make the going tough
So exploit this heavenly gift
Then lots of troubles we could shift.

Harry Derx

Notes

I am 46 years old, the eldest of five children, from a mining family.

I have been married to Susan for 25 years and we have two children, Sally and Christopher. I live in Chesterfield and I am employed as a Community Care Worker. I was unemployed several times before gaining my BA Honours degree and qualification in Social Work.

I have been writing poetry for approximately sixteen years and this is the second time I have been published. I am inspired to write when the mood *takes me*.

My hobbies include: reading, walking, politics and bird-watching.

Susan

Your spirit surrounds me like a blanket of love
Your warmth sustains me like the sun
You bring me happiness on the darkest day
Long may I cherish your love this way.

Day after day, year after year
Until the end of our time
I'll be there with love for you
To bring you comfort and cheer

Like a restless spirit in an ever changing world
You bring stability to my life.
Your talents are surely heaven sent
No mere mortal could please me so

Let's travel together down life's highway
to reach our final goal
With you I want to die in peace
Hand in hand together always

David Fox

Notes

This poem was written for a dear friend of mine who is now a well known face on British TV due to the continuing success of 'Aussie' Soaps here. An established stage actress and television Star in Australia, I was privileged to have worked and struck up a close friendship with her during my stay in Australia in the sixties. In those days we were both struggling Thespians. The poem says the rest.

For Judy Blue

I sipped my coffee from a polystyrene cup
And the dregs hung dark and dusty
as I spoke to her.
I asked if she knew someone
with whom I'd worked so far away.
Was she doing well?
Were things all right?
From here I couldn't tell.

She looked at me and sipped her coffee too
'Do you know her?' she asked.
I nodded 'yes.'
Then she said: 'Well I don't.
Us extras are kept in a corral, see.
No where near the 'stars',
Only in shoots.
No, I've never met her. Sorry.'

I looked back at the dregs in my coffee cup,
then up at the lights and the drapes hanging
so limp and lonely there.
My mind flew away twelve thousand miles
And I stood beside you on that empty street.
'Reckon we'll make it?' you asked.
''Course we will,' I answered.
And you did.

Terence G Ward

Thoughts From the Beach

Oh that you were here, my love
To share this scene of pure delight
With dancing waves that tease the shore
As day rolls gently into night

A bluer sea I doubt you'll find
Or softer sand than that I tread
The evening sun is calling me
To free the thoughts inside my head

I leave my tracks, in lonely state
To be erased by tide and time
I leave my dreams and hope one day
To see your footsteps next to mine

Anne Wheble

You

You - who I thought I knew quite well
Have taken my breath away.
You have surprised me
to the point that my emotions have runneth over.
You have taken my breath away.

I am now left with a newly found cave
in which to explore.
What treasures are there to be found?
You are an undiscovered lake.
You are virgin snow.
You - have taken my breath away!

You - who I thought I knew quite well
Have a radiance about you.
You have let the light in on my darkness
So that I can see again.
You have taken my breath away.

Lee Allen

Notes

Alice Benson is an ac-
tress/writer/poet. Perform-
ing her own work at various
venues.

A direct descendant of writer
E F Benson, famous for his
series of Mapp and Lucia
books. Alice is also a descen-
dant of the poet Fredrich Von
Schiller.

What is Life Without You, is
the first poem she ever wrote,
and the second to be pub-
lished. It was written shortly
after her mother died. It was
the first time she wrote her
feelings down in verse form,
and the start of her writing
many more poems. *Therefore
this poem is dedicated to Al-
ice's mother.*

What is Life Without You?

What is life without you?
Please will someone tell.
On the surface I am smiling,
inside I feel like hell.

I wish you were still here,
to guide me through the day.
There's so much I'd love to tell you,
so much I long to say.

Why is life and love so empty,
without you by my side,
I just want to leave all this,
and run away and hide.

Unfairness, hurt and pain,
are with me all the day.
At times I come across as hard,
I keep all love at bay.

Sometimes my smile is covering pain,
wishing life wasn't so empty again.
I laugh, but I feel my heart might break.
Wishing you would be back when I awake.

I live for my dreams, never wishing to wake,
unless dreams can come true, and my heart it won't break.

To lose a Mother, is a pain like no other.

Alice Benson

Notes

I live in Birmingham and am married with four children and seven grandchildren. When I was bringing my children up I wrote as a freelance journalist on women's issues, safety and consumer topics.

I have always liked reading poetry aloud and first started writing poems in my teens. I started writing again five years ago in my sixties. My poems are triggered by strong memories and emotions. The images haunt me obsessively until I can get them down on paper.

The Embrace

That day we walked to the parked car
She turned and said, 'Give me a big hug.'
Out in the street I embraced her.
Her bones softened - she was small within my arms;
Then, straightening up, she drove me to the station.

On the train home I could not remember
When we had last hugged;
Kissed yes - a peck on the cheek.
But years ago when she arrived by train
She'd step from the carriage, ready with arms apart
For us to rush to an embrace . . .

Years ago, and not again until
That day when we walked to the parked car:
It was the last time I saw her;
She died a week later.

Now I too spread welcoming arms
To husband, grandchildren,
Arriving friends; it may be
Our last day together.

Cynthia Walton

Our World

Notes

*Dedicated to R whom I loved
so dearly. (Carpe Diam)*

It is so hard
When two persons in love are pulled apart
Each life seems empty, incomplete,
A wandering body bereft of its heart.

Nothing can compensate for the stolen happiness
Which they shared in secret,
Hidden away from the eyes of the world
Their own guarded domain which cannot be entered,
Cannot be touched, cannot be shared.
A world for which they, and only they cared.

They fled to their world where time could stand still
Their love spoke out openly
Growing each day, growing in strength
Each one expressing the dreams to fulfil.

Such love never was, and never will be again
A love which was true, a love which was pure
A love full of hope; they really were sure
Their love could never die.

But their world was invaded
It came to an end so swiftly
No chance to say goodbye
To kiss farewell or say 'I will try
To return, if only in your dreams, I will be there.'

Time has passed slowly
One tries to return to the world which was lost
Empty of feeling, no comfort, no joy
The enemy cry is 'Destroy, destroy!
We cannot allow this love to live.'

But true love conquers all
And I will be there when you seek out our world
My presence with you will be felt in your heart
Return to those places where we dreamed our dreams
In 'our world' they never can keep us apart.

You'll feel my closeness, you'll feel my touch
So gentle and loving
And I will caress you as oft' times before
'Though you may not see me, believe I am there
Today and forever, and how I will share
With you, our precious love
When we meet again in the heavens above.

Charles V Swallow

For A

Through twenty years no day has passed
When I've not thought of you
And wondered at what might have been.
For all I know I might have passed
You in the street just yesterday -
I should not know you now.
Too many years have passed -
Though still I see your face of long ago,
And you would wonder vaguely who I was.
I know you never thought of me
Though I cannot forget.

Pauline Kontani

The Five Senses

(for Clare)

Rose-fingered dawn, do not just yet, I pray,
Announce the coming of another day:
My love and I, we have no use for light,
But want you to prolong this magic night.

Is it in darkness that a kiss tastes best?
We never cease to put this to the test
And, when out lips meet for the hundredth time,
No taste in all the world is more sublime.

She needs no light, my love, to clearly hear
The sweet words that I whisper in her ear.
Its absence multiplies the entrancing joy,
She gives me with her softly laughing voice.

Set not the intrusive sun up in the sky,
While in my sweetheart's slender arms I lie
And gently stroke her shoulder's luscious curve,
Which sets aglow - again - my every nerve.

I breathe the enticing perfume of her skin,
Her hair and all her fragrance feminine.
We share the air, in blindness I inhale
the honey of her mouth, my Holy Grail.

No one restrains Apollo's chariot:
That time goes by is our predestined lot.
Wake up my love! The sun! Come see it rise . . .
Whilst I watch its reflection in your eyes.

A Noltes

Notes

I am 83, a retired Anglican priest, living in Bognor Regis. I have published three books of light verse entitled *Rhyme and Rhythm for Relaxation*. I use my word processor to set them up and send them to Intype, Wimbledon, to Photostat and bind them. They are popular locally where they sell at £3.50.

At present I am revising a two act musical play that I wrote years ago and am also working on an English grammar book in verse, covering basic principles for eleven year old children. I am looking for a publisher for this.

The Robin

(A Good Friday Legend)

They took our Lord to Calvary
To hang Him on a tree,
And the angels wept in Heaven
His suffering to see.

Then they nailed Him to its branches
As cruelly as could be,
And the angels wept in Heaven
His agony to see.

A crown of thorns they plaited Him
With savage mocking glee,
And the angels wept in Heaven
Such wickedness to see.

The sharp thorns pierced the loving head
Of Him who died for me,
And the angels wept in Heaven
His sacrifice to see.

Then Gabriel sent some little birds
To pluck those sharp thorns free,
And the angels smiled in Heaven
Those small brown birds to see.

Christ's blood upon each tiny breast
Was red as red could be,
And the angels gazed in wonder
At such a sight to see.

So all robins' breasts are scarlet
Throughout eternity,
And the angels sing in Heaven
To hymn their gallantry.

C Champneys Burnham

Notes

I wrote this poem quite a few years ago now, and since then it has been modified here and there. I don't really know what it is about, I suppose it's about a housewife tucked away in suburbia with hopes that she cannot see being fulfilled.

I am 23 years old and live in Manchester. I've had a couple of other poems published with Poetry Today and Poetry Now. I have a degree in Geography and I hope to return to University to take a Masters degree in 1997.

The Forgotten Woman

Look at this face and say what you see
Is it Love? Is it Pain? Is it Free?
Look at this life - the woman it holds
And think whether you do love me.

Look at my hands, the work that they do
Remember the touch that they give
But as you are thinking, remember one thing
I have my own live to live.

Look at my writing, study the words
Follow the tale that is told
But shyness takes over, I keep things within
Never could I be so bold.

Look at me closely - see me inside
Look at this life that I lead
And though you don't notice my mind and my soul
You must see it's just you that I need.

Look at me now as the years have gone by
Look at the hope that's inside
Try to remember the times that I cared
And know that at least I have tried.

When I look back on this in the time still to come
Will I laugh? Will I cry? Will I see?
When I think of the days that I truly adored you
Will I know that you truly loved me?

Sarah V Deakin

The Upside-Down Smile

Notes

For Tori - my love, my light, my friend.

Furrowing for luscious ripe strawberries in nettled pastures
With the sun on my back,
Cutting through leaden clouds with blunt dreams,
Seeing the rainbow's upside-down smile,
Bathing in your ocean blue eyes.

Feeling the power of a race car with no brakes,
Tearing round chicanes with no bends,
At night,
Stealing a thousand glances per hour.

A season passing in a day,
Today those trees cried for you
Along a boulevard,
Tasting the flavour of your delicious voice.

Playing the piano with my heart
Under the stars,
To a quickening pulse which plays a samba rhythm.

Holding you close with my thoughts,
Drying your tears in advance,
Lounging in the luxury of your smile;
Is what falling in love is like.

Liam Wells

If You Should Learn to Love Me

Notes

This poem was written for my wife, shortly after we met. She was divorced after her first marriage, which had been very traumatic, and found it hard to contemplate giving her love and trust to any man. I wrote it to say that I understood and was happy to wait until she was sure of her feelings.

We have now been married, very happily, for just over eight years.

If you should ever find that you have learned to love me
And that you feel the need to tell me,
Let it not be when you are in my arms
And you can see the love in my eyes,
Nor as our lips are parting or meeting;
Nor at some quiet romantic moment,
But on a crowded street, in the pouring rain,
At the end of a long day,
When there appears to be no reason
Why you should love anyone,
And least of all me.
Turn to me then, hold me close
And softly whisper, 'I love you.'

Richard Young

Fate

Notes

I am a 49 year old ex-
computer engineer who has
suffered from manic depres-
sion for the last ten years.
During that time I have
written a number of poems,
something I never did before
my illness. *Fate* was written
after a very significant dream
along with three other poems
at the time.

Of all the girls I ever had
Made me happy made me sad
It was you at last that I chose
Eastern pearl not English rose

Each could have had another mate
But you cannot alter fate
Who decides our lives well ahead
From the cradle to the deathbed

Our paths were meant to cross some day
For what purpose who can say
But cross they did and so they'll be
Till our souls can wander free

The greatest time in all my life
Was when you said you'd be my wife
A gift more precious and worth
More than all the gold on earth

I hope there'll never come the day
When we ever have to say
Goodbye because we've lost all sight
Of why you dressed all in white

Charlie Wolf

Untitled

Notes

This poem was written for a lady whose name I cannot mention. Her name was replaced by the words Shayne Madel, Yiddish for beautiful maiden. My relationship with her has been very strange, but I hope this poem sums it up.

If I cock my head, I can hear your voice.
Your lovely, gentle, whispering voice.
The voice that carries all the pain in the world.
Your beautiful soft-lined face.
Filled with far too much hurt.
That face was made for laughing, Shayne Madel.
Not for frowning or for tears.
Use me.
Fill me with your pain.
I can chew it up, make it happiness,
and give it back to you.
The only gift I have to give.
For though it honours me that you pick me
to tell me of your pain.
It would make me feel so much happier
If you could share with me your joy.

Michael Toper

Love ~ Second Time Around

He'd have to be good I can tell you,
With a drill, a paintbrush and saw,
'Cos the bathroom handle's falling off
And we've flooded the kitchen floor.

The garden to put it mildly
Like a jungle aims to be,
Whilst the garage is full of clapped-out cars,
So I'd need mechanic, you see.

I'd really expect him to get busy
At once with rewiring the house,
And have enough bottle to remove
The remains of the cat's dead mouse.

Let's hope he'd like loud music
Since my sons like it only too well;
But three different kinds played together?
It's a cacophony created in hell.

And cooking? He'd need a strong stomach
As burnt spaghetti's my favourite treat,
Dished up with a bolognaised sausage
Cooked over too great a heat.

Could there be so perfect a paragon
For a woman past her prime?
With her stomach no longer tight and flat
And whose breasts feel the forces of time?

Of course there is: For this morning
As I plastered the cracks in my face,
He bent, kissed me and said 'I love you'
Then went down to restore order and grace!

Christine Barham

Love Poem

My love I must tell you of how it would be
If the moon were to dream of a face she would see
Some of it golden, and some timid white
To lie in the lap of a midsummer night.

The night would be staggered and the moon she would cry
Then lean low with a whisper of silver and sigh
For the kiss of the wind that had gathered to stare
Is the blood and the bones and the flame of your hair

And when the cold and the gold had oozed upward
Through the moist and the mortal air
When the worlds and the winds had gathered
To flower and flow through your hair.
When the flesh of the forest had stirred
Some faith in these pagan dreams
Then I'd know that God was a woman
As the earth is a mother to me.

Simon Brian Cartlidge

Swimming

A great warm feeling
Swelling up from inside.
Calm, reassuring,
Like a midsummer's tide.

Add a surge of want;
An overpowering need
To make a connection
Where my soul can feed.

Drawn to the place
where replenishment is,
Naked and hungry
I want what is his.

To soothe this ache
To fill this gap
to feel the force
That is life's sap.

I chase the heat
The Chase is fast,
- I want it to happen:
But also to last.

My body shudders
He releases the flow
The tension eases
We relax for the glow.

Content and calm
I love him so much
Safe in his arms
Where no one can touch

Then we can talk
About this and about that
It's the easy contentment
That is lover's chat.

Slowly the blanket
Of night fills the sky,
As we sleep the deep sleep,
My lover and I

G McAnee

Notes

Born on 11 August 1951 in Pennsylvania, USA. Married in England to Don in August 1994 - without whose encouragement and love my writing could not be possible.

This poem is dedicated to my eldest son Justin. It is the key to life. It is all that I have learned, and I give it to you.

The Important Things in Life

Love of God
Love of Man
The ability to appreciate beauty
The desire to create it
The patience to enjoy it
The willingness to share it
The compulsion to give it away

Suzette Wynder

The Reason for Being

Notes

My name is Mike Crampton.
I am 30 years old, and I live
in England's most beautiful
city, York.

I have been writing poetry
for about ten years now, and
I find it is a good way of
clearing a lot of the cobwebs
from your soul. this is my
second poem published by
Poetry Today.

*The reason for being, is dedi-
cated to, and written for
Kelly, my one, my only, my
love.*

To all else do I seem,
as a man, alone and proud,
one who scorns not a charitable cause,
yet who kneels to no one.
But to you, do I come
as I truly am,
as one haunted by a vision so perfect,
that all else is merely smoke from a fire,
drifting on the breeze
of a summer evening.
You smile, and I laugh,
you weep, and my tears are falling rain,
you love, and I am yours forever.
If my life were to end,
I would that it ended here,
for if I could not live in your grace,
I should wish to die in no company
but yours.
My warrior's heart,
is yours, and yours alone,
none could tear your love
from my body,
or your face from my eyes.
You are my soul.
You are my passion.
Light in my darkest night,
my soul dances
to the music of your existence.

Mike Crampton

Notes

In the past eighteen months I have written around fifty poems and *Wolf in Sheep's Clothing* is my second to be published by Poetry Today.

I am at the moment trying to produce my own poetry book called *Sacred Emotions* which is a mix of different poems that range from love and hate to joy and despair but they are all about my life.

I have always enjoyed writing and shall continue to write for as long as I can.

I live in Christchurch, Dorset with my family who enjoy and support my writing.

I would like to dedicate this poem to my mum and step dad who I love very much and without their confidence in me and my poems I would never have continued writing.

Wolf in Sheep's Clothing

I should have known,
It wasn't true love,
Like I'd wanted it,
From heaven above.

I should have realised
They are all the same.
They take your for granted
Then forget your name.

How can he be so selfish and cruel.
I thought he was different
But it can't be renewed.

I feel so abused like nobody cares,
I feel so abandoned when everyone stares.

I fell for him, heart, body and soul,
Completely in love, now I'm in a deep hole.

He's a wolf in sheep's clothing,
Or that's how it seems
I thought that he loved me
But that's only in my dreams.

Kathryn Long

What is Love?

Love is intangible, so hard to define
The boundary of love is a very fine line.
When we say I love you, just what do we mean?
It's something we feel, not something that's seen.
It's tenderness and warmth, understanding and caring,
It's the epitome of unselfishness, the joy in sharing
It's wanting your loved one beside you each day,
Not mutually exclusive, it's better that way.
It's your loved one declaring the thoughts in your head,
It's your loved one suggesting it's time we were wed
It's knowing each day, he'll be there at your side
Just as sure as the ebb and the flow of the tide
And when in our lives this loves come to call
Its joy and its spirit will capture us all

Susan E Hallett

Home

I see your face in the crowd
my heart turns over I feel so proud.
I knew you once I loved you so
oh why did I let you go

You turn around and catch my eye
you walk towards me I give a sigh
you smile at me, you look pleased
I remember that smile, it was the one that teased.

My heart beats fast it misses a beat
then suddenly you're standing at my feet.
You take my hand look into my eyes
my heart soars I'm, in paradise

You're arms slip around me and hold me tight
I can hardly breathe but it's all right
I lay my head upon your chest
these are the arms that I love best.

You trace my mouth with your fingertips
then you touch it with your lips
I missed you so when you were away
and I have longed for this day

Now you're back by my side
never to leave again with the tide.
On dry land forever my sailor O'
my darling husband, I love you so.

Helen Arthur

Notes

Usually I prefer my poetry to rhyme, but I decided I would try my hand at writing blank verse, and the poem *My Love* was the result. Being rather ancient in years, and having just visited a shop specialising in modern bathrooms, the theme of young passion symbolised by a swirling Jacuzzi, contrasted with the cool stillness of a calm pool symbolising love in old age became the subject of the poem.

My Love

My love was like a jacuzzi
Bubbling, sparkling, effervescent,
A hidden source of passion,
Eager, vibrant. A hidden spring
Of energy. Perpetual, undiminishing
Waves of desire, encroaching,
Like a moon-led tide.
Romantic, dark, fervent.
A source of mystery, renewal,
And a restless motion.

My love is like a tranquil pond,
Unchanging, endless, satisfying,
A hidden source of calm.
Soothing, lasting. A hidden pool
Of peace. Healing, sustaining,
Echoing fond memories, restful,
With warm, enfolding arms.
Quiet, revealed and softly grey,
A source of sweet repose. Undying,
With a deep contentment.

Jack Scrafton

I penned this poem some several years after the Aberfan disaster. I was one of the people helping at this disaster on the morning it happened. I did not write it to bring back the terrible memories for the families concerned but just to remind the people who were in authority then

To Remember

I was 60 years old on 4th September 1997. I have a son Christopher, who is 36 years old and a daughter who is 28 years old. She is married and lives in Brisbane, Australia. Her names are Dawn Caroline. Caroline being my late mother's name. My daughter also writes beautiful poetry.

I am a retired HGV driver, and my hobbies are carving and making walking sticks and watching nature unfold. Most of my poetry is written from true life experiences and their happenings over my lifetime. I have never had any works published.

Inspiration for my poetry and writing lie in nature's marvels and also all of its conservation.

I hope you can glean some ideas and thoughts about my background from this short essay of my life and family.

Remember the Heartbreak and Strife

With the warm summer sun shining bright in my face
I walked to the top of the hill
And I looked all around and I listened to sound:
I swallowed the black, bitter pill:
Wheeling high overhead was a hawk in the sky:
And I wondered at what he could see
Did he think of the now green mountainside,
Or did he think of that black tragedy?

I thought of the times when I sat with my Dad,
And I asked him questions now answered,
Of huge pointed tips that reach to the sky,
Of beautiful valleys black cancered,
Of men who were told not once but tenfold
Of some who would pay with their life;
But they didn't heed, it was money and greed:
Remember the heartbreak and strife.

I looked to the now green valley below,
At the river, a bright silver ribbon;
I thought of the lives that men took away,
I thought of the life God had given:
If only they knew just what they would do
When they spewed up this black from the ground,
And I wonder sometimes does it run through their minds,
Was it worth it for green paper pounds?

Though the years quickly pass I must say it, alas,
Men will just go on being too greedy,
But don't let them forget the terrible debt
Of hearts left lonely and needy,
Of a terrible day that once came our way
And I know that you'll pray if you can
That these men will take heed, forget money and greed:
Please God - no more black Aberfan.

G Cleeves

Notes

What is love? was written at a time when I was involved in a wonderful, loving partnership. Sadly, we are no longer together, but rather than dwell on the pain of separation, I can't help but draw upon the enchanting happy memories. Still vivid and fresh in my heart is the sheer rapture and magic of the moment we met outside a phone box in Liverpool, the day we got engaged, but most of all, when she turned to me and asked, 'What is Love?'

What is Love?

Is love a mere fantasy, a conscientious lust;
    The idealism of society, or unconditional trust;
Benevolence of the heart, or aspirations of the mind;
    Love is easy now, but so often fades with time.

Love creates fulfilment, but exists so close to hate;
    A sacred test of time, of how long a heart can wait,
Everything you need, to enhance your very soul;
    The destiny of our love, with time will yet unfold.

Is love within my life, or is love yet to live?
    Is love a mere reflection, of how much I long to give;
A presence that surrounds as, so abstract yet so real;
    All I know within myself, is the love you make me feel.

Simon Hoffman

Lost Love

There's a strange light outside my window
that turns night into day
but it hovers just beyond my reach
since you went away.
The emptiness I sometimes feel
keeps the warmth away from me,
and the darkness and the cold creep in
like a well-known enemy.

I know that I can't have you
I never thought I could.
Nor that I ever really did.
Nor that I ever should.
But I should like to be a bird
soaring high and free,
so that I could reach that strange, warm light
to bring you back to me!

Patricia Nickle

Untitled

Sure! Love is blind,
It won't penetrate my mind,
I have two cataracts and a dog
But it's love that's blind.

Sure love is blind!
Once, it skimmed the edges of my mind,
I looked but didn't see
Through my rose-coloured glasses,
Now I take the consequences.

Evelyn Voigt

Notes

This poem was written for, and dedicated to my wife Brida at our wedding in September 1996. It was read out as part of the service. One year on it still applies.

I am glad it was chosen to be part of *Mixed Emotions* as this is the ultimate show of affection to Brida, to have this poem published.

Love forever.

You are My World

You are my world
My setting sun.
You're a picture
Like the dawn begun.
Lighting my life
So I can see,
A new found hope
In front of me.
A glowing smile
Upon your face,
But an empty bed
Surrounding the space.
A knowing look
Glistens in your eye
Whenever we're apart
It's never goodbye.
My life is nearly complete
Now I've found you,
So don't you worry now
Because this love is true.

Simon Weatherer

The Eternal Candle

As long as the sun appears in the sky so bright,
and the moon shines in the dead of night.
I will love you.

The moon shines each and every night,
surrounded by thousands of stars so bright.
The time it would take to count each and every one.
I will still love you.

The time it would take to travel
the deepest depths of the universe,
going from star to star or travelling
on a passing meteor.
I will still love you.

An eternity is all time forever,
forever and a day,
as long as I breathe,
You will hold that special place in my heart,
my soul and my mind,
for I will always love you.

J Reay

Love Birds

I'm always blue
please be true
My darling love
we're like two turtle doves
Flying in the air
Like a perfect pair.

Julie Paton

Trust

Notes

This poem I wrote for my partner Alan, when we were forced to be apart for more than a year during a family crisis and I tried not to give up hope.

My love, shall we walk
Along the beach, follow the road?
Then I'll listen while you talk,
Lightening your heavy load.
Hands in mine 'neath darkening sky
Trying to explain
While whispering waves, rolling by
Might wash away our pain.

Tell me softly of your fears,
Know there's nothing you can't say
All your worries, and my tears,
The sea will carry them away.
Watch them swiftly disappear,
Flowing with the tide,
To a place so far from here
Where they go, to hide.

Come with me, view from above,
My freedom bird in flight,
While I show you how our true love
Soars up to greater height.
Waves of woe will be no more:
The sea has sworn to give,
With waves of joy that flow ashore,
A great new life to live

Pauline Smith

To My Valentine

To my Valentine on this special day
Our love for each other is here to stay

My love for you grows more and more
Your my very special person of which I adore

Valentine's Day comes but once a year
All year round I love you most dear
Love for you is always in my heart
Every day we're together, never apart
Now on Valentine's Day I send you my love
To you from me from way up above
I love you now and I'll love you forever
Now and forever
Each day we're together

Belinda Pyett

Notes

I have written this poem from my heart. With love and devotion. May true love never die. May it last forever, like a flame may it burn. May love be there until the end.

My Loved One

I see such beauty in your eyes
Clearer than the summer skies.
I touch your hand
Caress your face
Please come with me
To a special place.
Where I can sing you songs of love
Come share with me the stars above.
Your beauty burns me with desire
That fills me like a burning fire.
Please listen to these words I say
Near me may you always stay.
You are to me a precious thing
Just like a lark
My heart does sing.
Like a jewel set in a crown
You take away each tear and frown.
These words I give only to you
My dearest one
I love so true.

Delyse Healey-Proctor

Taboo

There's something about sex that's completely taboo,
yet it can't be done without me and you!
What is it that's so scary?
That makes everybody wary
of saying what they don't like
and especially what they do!

Chantal Dent

Is it Wrong to Speak of Love?

Is it wrong to speak of love
In cities far away?
Or any worse to test your heart
When, having spent so long apart,
I cannot find the words to say
And weep into my glove?

Ceri Stafford

Notes

I feel at this time in my life, I have to express myself, through my poems. This is *me* and I will do my utmost to give people pleasure in my work. Thank you, everyone.

Secret Love

How can anyone tell, or show what love is
My heart beats my beloved when we only kiss
Sweet words pour from one's lips into each other
Rain, winds, sunshine, leaves fall and rush by, we don't bother
Your hands caress my breasts making my blood pound
As you kiss around my neck, you slowly bear me to the ground
The world rushes by, and daytime turns into night
As your naked body lies on mine your maleness gives me delight
All too soon my beloved, hearts aching, we go our separate ways
For fate is unkind to us my one and only true love
As we share our secret days.

Gwendoline Byrne

Misplaced Love

Turn down your heart
Open your hands
Listen to love
Take it by the hand,
Show me all that's good in your soul
I'll do al I can
To reach this goal.

You don't have to cry
To prove to me
That all in my life
Is not what it seems,
I feel the same things that you do.
If you look at me
You'd feel them too

Close your eyes, slip away,
Let the night subdue this fire
Love is the stranger in my bed
I feel nothing but anger
You lied and I'm dead

Time will again come round
Love will spring
Smiles will walk on my face
Happy will me embrace

I was happy in the womb
Nothing but room
I cling now to strands of natal mucous
I cannot despair no longer
I am heading for the tomb
Love you? Not in this world.

Tony McKenzie

Love

Love is a willowy wispy thing.
Love is a bird on the wing.
Love is joy to give to others
The sun of your life,
The dew of your tears.

Reaching forth
From the dim dark past,
Preaching the truth
To those who have lost.

Finding the key to a
Radiant hour,
Enclosed in the sunset of
Sweet desire.

Mind to mind
And heart to heart
Only those who have loved
Can know its power.

Priscilla Clough

Be With Me

Notes

This poem was written to a girl I loved very much. she was leaving to go back to Australia and I wrote this so she would remember the times we had together.

For every single day that passes by
I long to relive that natural high
because that's how I feel when I'm with you
I know I love you, I know it's true
Whenever you're near you have that look in your eye
I wish I could hold you till the day that I die
You're just so beautiful and always so kind
There's not a minute goes by, when you're not on my mind

I wish we could be, together as one
And live our lives in perpetual sun
Swim in the ocean, make love on the beach
I'd take you higher than you ever could reach
So take all these thoughts into consideration
when I come to see your wonderful nation
for I love you so much and this is how I feel
And as long as I live, you'll know it's for real.

David Crowe

The fragility of life is what makes it worth living.

Dedicated to the girl with the kaleidoscope eyes.

Special Times

(Another Love Poem)

Now I understand the words from the love songs
As my heart bellows strong emotions like silver gongs.
Rivers of emotions meet the sea of my beating heart
Only the Gods can see my pain until the love game slowly starts
Air is no longer needed for me to survive one more day
Just you by my side, holding my hand, keeping sad emotions away
The sun is in your shadow when you are awake
The moon at night, when compared to you, is nothing but a fake
Your soul captures mine and sets it alight
Attack all the sorrow to win the love fight
I'm only whole when near to you, sweet flower
From this day forth you're the one with all the power
The roses weep when they see your beautiful eyes
Everyone else looks and unconsciously flies high

As the bells of my soul chime
I realise these are truly special times.

David John Bell

For my husband and dear children

How Do I Feel About You My Love

The first snowflake to fall in winter.
The joy of the newly born lamb in spring.
The warmth of the summer sun.
The golden coloured leaves in autumn.
This is how I feel about you my love.
You are all things and all seasons.
You are my life, laughter and joy.
You are my reason for living.
You are my forever love, my love.

Siobhan OConchubhair

Nearly Perfect

It was nearly perfect, you and I
Hazy magical days, steamy sensual nights
Every nerve on fire,
Passions punctuated by palpitations of reality

Dreamy walks home,
Mourning for what should be,
The pain immense,
For the love that I desire,
But will never gain.

Why love if losing means so much
Because discomfort is its essence
And without that pain,
We are nothing,
And without you
I'll never be complete.

Stephen McAllister

Notes

I'm nearly 16 and currently
in my fifth year at Byrchall
High School, Ashton-in-
Makerfield. I have written
many poems but this is the
second one I have had pub-
lished. I have been writing
poems in my spare time for
three years.

Forget Him

Forget his name,
Forget his face,
Forget his kiss,
His warm embrace,
Forget the love you once knew,
Remember he has someone new,
Forget him when they play your song,
Forget you cried the whole night long,
Forget how close you two once were,
Remember he has chosen her.

Debbie Daniels (15)

Mother's Day 1996

*This poem is dedicated to my
mother.*

I am part of a close knit fam-
ily and feel that Mother's Day
is a time when the family
should be together, unfortu-
nately because we live so far
apart this is not possible.

I wrote this poem to let her
know that I love her and my
feelings can be felt through
words no matter how many
miles there are between us.

I miss you more and more each day
I wish you weren't so far away
I wonder when you'll be close to me
I long for the day that shall be.

I didn't really want you to know
that I am feeling so low
I need to let this message flow
to show you how I miss you so.

I really want to have you near
to show you that I love you dear
to chase away that nagging fear
so together we can shed a happy tear.

The miles that keep us far apart
puts an extra pull on my heart
I wish we could be close together
to share the love we have for each other.

Ann May

You are Mine

Light as the spring blown breeze through catkins
A feathery caress is yours to me,
As though not touching, but there forever

Bright as a new unfolding fern on quiet common
Your smile conveys a cosy warmth,
Mine to hold until eternity

Pure as the lilt of soaring lark on high
Your love and endearing faith are mine,
Taken often lightly, such is my pity

Truer than the crossbow shaft of Tell
Your sincere devotion to my being,
I, sometimes thoughtless, will ever adore you.

L R Pearce

She Knows

To Tracey, with all my love

Her skin, soft to touch,
Her lips, inviting,
Her arms, warming,
Her thoughts, inspiring.
Her smile, encouraging,
Her laugh, captivating,
Her eyes, all knowing,
Her tears, stomach churning.

Her absence, annoying,
Her halves', mocking,
Her look, loving,
Her words, caring.

Of time . . .
there is never enough with her
there is too much without.

Derek Harte

Notes

I am 37 years old and live in
Worcester.

This poem was inspired by
the break-up of my marriage
and the subsequent soul
searching that followed.

I have written poetry for the
past 20 years; initially as lyr-
ics for bands in which I
played. Today poetry is a way
of relieving inner tensions
without going into a self-
destruct mode which could
be easy in stressful times.

The Rose

That rose that is given as a love token is like love in itself,
As a bud it is so tight and firm, all its life squeezed into such a small space,
Two kindred souls engrossed in one another, with underlying stealth,
The sparkling fresh eyes, the beaming smiles, the glowing of a face,
Brings joy to the hearts of those involved, in every given way,
Sharing untold stories, hopeful for the future, dreams of days to come,
Plans of distance times, places to see, so many words to say,
So close that hope springs to unchanging moods for some.

Time has passed with its usual ease, the rose is blooming the lushest red,
Like the colour the fragrance is so intense, fills the air with a heady scent,
Love is at ease with itself, confidence between the parts, although fewer
                                                            words said,
Shape and form are beauty in themselves, although less time is spent,
With each other, true love holding the rose in a timeless design,
Showing to the world, and all that want to see, the finest thing of life,
The truth is still there, the feeling is right, and all in life is fine,
With all being so well there should be no easy place for strife.

For every rose we hope this blooming will last forever,
Those happy times, the joyful heart, the confidence in what is good,
But even the hardiest plant can be overcome by stormy weather,
Easy to fall foul of familiarity, things not being as they should,
The petals begin to become discoloured and slowly wither away,
Some fall from their rightful place, others become hard and dry,
The water becomes murky, cloudy with freezing fog of a winter day,
The love that was a beautiful tight bud, without care will one day surely
                                                            die.

Clive Message

Notes

On this particular day frustration is too often the name of the game. Anticipation and dreaming are sometimes the chosen remedies - hence this poem - and I'm still waiting for my door-bell to ring!

A Perfect Valentine

Whilst sitting by my fireside,
When Valentine's comes round,
To hear the door-bell ringing
Would make my heart-strings pound,
For, it could mean the waiting
For the one I've longed to see
Has ended, and you've come to say,
That you have need of me?

Just three lovely little words
Would tell me why you came,
Translated by a loving heart,
As you whisper, 'Je vous aime.'
Sweet music to these ears of mine;
The truly perfect Valentine.

S Stafford

Notes

This poem is for those whom
seek love, for those whom
have found love and for those
whom have known love.

*Dedicated to Darrin, Karen,
my Granddaughter, Aimèe,
Leigh and my daughter,
Leeann.*

What is Love?

Love is found in many places,
Love has many different faces,
Love is caring and sharing,
Love is trusting and giving and seeking no other.

The love for a wife, a husband, a friend,
Is a different kind of love than that felt by a mother.
Love should be unconditional.

If you find love nurture and protect it,
It is a gift from one to another,
Love, like a piece of precious glass,
Can be shattered by a hurtful deed or word,
And may never be mended.

Love each other then while you may,
Don't let your love be a memory from the past,
Treasured memories are made to last.

Marilyn McLeod Wilson

Angel, My Shining Star

Two hearts devoted to each other
during life and death.
She will never be replaced by another,
Her kiss took away my breath.

Now she's looking down on me from the sky,
She might even be a shining star,
Sometimes it breaks me to cry,
love so close, yet so far.

Half a man, broken in two.
The days pass, though I don't seem to care.
She had a beautiful soul, one of a few,
How it did shine, here, there and everywhere.

Sometimes I wish I was in a dream,
I'd wake up and taste the taste from her lips
As fresh as a mountain stream,
My love, how my heart it strips.

Someday I will feel her again
and smell her hair across my cheek,
I'm dying slowly with pain,
loneliness, week after week.

Her look is trapped in me forever,
That picture will not fade or wither.
I could stare at her, and feel her touch,
and my heart, love would clutch.

Angels come take me away,
And with her I will stay.

R McMullan

Say You do . . .

I long to see you
to tell you
everything I feel inside
to tell you I love you
and want you near me
always
I don't think you like me
tho' you say you do
Please reassure me
Please
Life is nothing without you
People are empty
faces are misty
Nobody really knows me
or wants me
Say you do

Sally-Anne Warren

Notes

I am a 17 year old 'A' Level
student from Nottingham.

I have been published many
times in a local evening paper
and a local School newsletter.
This will be the sixth book I
have been published in.

The poem is self-explanatory,
about a man I loved a short
while ago.

I hope all who read it enjoy it
and can relate to it in some
way.

All I Wanted to Say

I loved our conversations.
I loved the way we chatted.
I loved the way you were there,
When it really mattered.
I loved your best dress suit,
And your wonderful tie.
I loved the way you looked at me;
It made me want to die.
I loved the way you watched,
And the way you listened.
I loved your amazing smile,
And the way your teeth glistened.
I loved it when you teased me.
I loved it when you stopped.
I loved the way you made me feel;
I always wanted to drop.
I loved your sense of humour,
And your honesty.
I loved the way you kissed my cheek;
You filled me up with glee.
I loved the way you wanted me,
My heart warmed through and through.
I guess all I wanted to say,
Is that, 'I loved you.'

Sarah Maher

Far Away Love

To touch, embrace,
To love, entwine,
To long to be together.

No one can know,
The pain we share,
Our love is there forever.

Maybe, one day,
Our love will get,
The chance to be our own.

Then we, can love
Each other more,
And never be alone.

Susan Amelia Chojecka

Notes

I am 28 years old, marred to Dominic and have two beautiful daughters, Charlotte, seven and Sophie, five. I live in Coleraine, northern Ireland.

I have been writing poetry for 20 years and have had other poems published entitled, *Erupted Love*, *Don't Let it be too Late*, *Power of Love*, *We are One* and *The Thistle*.

I am a very deep thinker, I love being mysterious and passionate. This poem was written to my husband, who is still trying to work out what goes on in my mind and soul.

Passionate Consumption

How mysterious you perceive me,
Blinded by my passionate soul,
Begging, feed my hunger,
Pleading, satisfy my all.
Look deep into my eyes,
Your mind, I'll transfix,
My spirit will shake you,
No impairment can be fixed.
Could you endure affinity,
Emancipate control,
Sustain unbearable pleasure,
Stay trapped for evermore.

Adele Norton

The Price of Love

Notes

The author was born on 24 September 1929, went through the war on a farm and was apprenticed as a welder in 1943 and served in HM forces for two years.

Now retired he is writing a column for the local evening paper, The South Wales Argus.

His hobbies include archery, writing, photography and local history.

'I was encouraged to write by my wife Joan, to whom I would like to dedicate this poem.'

We met while young, but still too late,
For I was wed, you could not wait,
And I was told 'It is not right,
that you should be out, every night,'
And friends who knew said 'While you play,
someone else will have to pay.'

But I would think 'I'm not a saint,
and love like this brooks no restraint,'
And always we would have our way,
regardless of the price to pay,
And friends we knew said at the start,
'You'll pay with someone else's heart.'

And we would often use those friends,
To further our own schemes and ends,
Others we loved would often say,
'There'll be a heavy price to pay,'
We did not care, they could not know,
We had to have somewhere to go.

But were those years lived out in vain?
With all their misery and pain?
We've paid our debt, and paid it all,
No debt collector need ever call,
Nor knowing looks from so-called friends,
Or poisoned letters they might send.

We paid the price, and it was high,
We did not want to live a lie,
But one thing's sure as heaven above,
We both now know the price of love.
But when I think the whole thing through,
I'd do it all again, for you.

G J Tilley

Sonnet

Shall I compare thee to a winter's night
When storms about the wind-shook belfry beat
And dark beneath the bitter freezing sleet
The road is hidden from Diana's light;
When violent gustings bend the poplars tall
And floods the rushing river o'er the weir;
When vole and shrew and spider shrink in fear
Along the cold and rain-soaked farmhouse wall?
I say thou art like such a storm to me
That hath laid waste the fortress of my heart
And like the hurricane no smallest part
Left of my secret soul untouched by thee;
      Yet I'd not have thee like a gentler time
      For summer rose hath ne'er won love of mine.

E J Mehta

Lost Love

The love I have,
In heart so strong,
Yet cannot show,
Always carries on.
Wake up the night,
Sleep in day,
My cry is still not heard,
Longing for happiness,
Inside so cold,
For a memory to live forever,
Once to all it was told,
When will it happen?
Never I fear,
For my love will grow.
Yet to all I know,
The sorrow is hidden inside,
A smile can hide all,
To the world out there,
Yet on the other side I cry,
Feeling so much pain,
Will I ever feel happiness again?

Amber Carter

Denial

I look through your eyes still constantly searching
For feelings of any kind that may still be lurking
Just waiting to surface when you can let go
Of the fear that you'll lose the control that you show
But surely that's not me but yourself you deceive
When you deny all those thoughts that involve you and me
The truth may be buried beneath grounds of deceit
But I know that your love and I will soon meet
That hard exterior may hide how you feel
But the cover of a book can only ever reveal
A small part of the story that lies beyond
And I have the patience to keep reading on
You can take a knife and sever our ties
But how can love be excused when it becomes apparent in your eyes?

Zöe Catlin

Captured

Captured in my love is rapture
Captured in my love is pain
Captured in my love is danger
with new feelings to proclaim
Captured in my love is craving
which my body strives to fill
Captured in my love is reward
where my lust will milk the pill
Captured in my love is betrayal
with guilt to mend the cost
Captured in my love is pity
when my innocence is lost
Captured in my love is trust
perching on a jagged hill,
Captured in my love is denial
when this host will not stay still
But captured in my love is warmth
when the fire burns inside
Captured in my love is music
As it dances with my pride

Emma McGhee

Perpetual Love

Peachy lips, gorgeous face
Such amazing
Big brown eyes
And your hands, they're so soft
When you touch
Sends a shiver down my spine
In the night, when you sleep
Close to me
Feel the beating of your heart
And your smell,
Redolence
Is an aphrodisiac of sort.

As the night seeps in, pulls the curtain to the land
Think of you
You're not there, my god makes me . . .
Sad is the look, on my face
When you're not there to hold my . . .
Hand *me your love, red velvet heart*
There's no safer place you'll . . .
Find the right time, the right place
To declare undying . . .
Love is *too short of a word*
To convey my hidden . . .
Thought, once or twice, that the note
'It's all over,' would be . . .
Wrote *out our script, dotted i's*
But to you I cannot send
'Cause our novel, throughout this life
Is not concluding with . . .

Jason Paul Mowbray

185

Spring Lives Because of You, is one of the poems that I wrote, to my husband Paul, whilst he was doing a six month tour in Bosnia, it helped me get over the lonely times, as well as to convey to my husband how I felt about him.

Spring Lives Because of You

The mist was thick as dawn came upon,
The trees were bare and scrawny,
My life reflected this imagery,
Until I came upon you,

Then spring came with showers of rain,
As life blossomed in every budding tree,

Our love grew great,
And the heavens could not wait,
As they vibrantly sang in chorus,
For the love that you give fills me,

And my smile blinds the sun,
For the love I have won,
And the love I give you openly.

T D Smith